Madonna The Immaculate Collection in Focus

by
Adrian York

Also available from Rhinegold Publishing:

Who's Next in Focus
Batman in Focus
Goldfinger in Focus
A Student's Guide to Music Technology for the Edexcel AS and A2 Specification
Listening Tests for Students for the Edexcel AS and A2 Specification

Rhinegold Study Guides:

Music
Music Technology
Classical Civilisation
Drama and Theatre Studies
Performance Studies
Religious Studies

Rhinegold Publishing also publishes Classical Music, Classroom Music, Early Music Today, Music Teacher, Opera Now, Piano, The Singer, Teaching Drama, British and International Music Yearbook, British Performing Arts Yearbook, Rhinegold Guide to Music Education, Rhinegold Dictionary of Music in Sound.

First published 2007 in Great Britain by
Rhinegold Publishing Ltd
241 Shaftesbury Avenue
London WC2H 8TF
Telephone: 020 7333 1720
Fax: 020 7333 1765
www.rhinegold.co.uk

You should always check the current requirements of the examination, since these may change. Copies of the Edexcel Specification may be obtained from Edexcel Examinations at Edexcel Publications, Adamsway, Mansfield, Nottinghamshire, NG18 4FN
Telephone: 01623 467467, Fax 01623 450481, Email publications@linneydirect.com
See also the Edexcel website at www.edexcel.org.uk

The Immaculate Collection in Focus
British Library Cataloguing in Publication Data.
A catalogue record for this book is available from the British Library.
ISBN: 978-1-906178-11-6
Printed in Great Britain by Thanet Press Ltd

Contents

The author

Adrian York started his professional career playing keyboards in the 80s band Roman Holliday. He then combined work as a session musician and musical director for a number of pop and jazz artists. In music education, Adrian was a professor at the Guildhall School of Music and Drama, and a visiting lecturer at the University of Westminster, London College Of Music, Brunel and Thames Valley Universities. He was a tutor at Brighton Rock, the Musicians' Union summer school, and he ran the Jazz FM Jazz Works school workshop programme, delivering more than 60 workshops in schools in the London area. Other education work includes contributing modules to the National Syllabus; training young bands to play at Buckingham Palace for the Prince's Trust; and his role as syllabus director for Rockschool.

Publications include articles in the *The Rockfile* (OUP 1991), and *The Cambridge Guide to Gospel and Blues* (CUP 2002), his own series of three books (*The Style File*, Music Sales), as well as articles for *Music Teacher* magazine.

For the last few years he has worked as a media composer with many credits in TV, radio and commercials. He also performs with artists including Mari Wilson, Claire Martin and Barb Jungr.

Acknowledgements

The author would like to thank Paul Tingen for digging out his copy of the *Sound on Sound* Patrick Leonard interview, and Rob Mounsey for his detailed email on the recording of *Crazy For You*. Most of all he thanks his three children – Lauren, Natalie and Louis – for keeping him entertained with their slick Madonna-style choreography, and his wife Bet for putting up with him. Thanks also to Hallam Bannister, Elizabeth Boulton, Chris Elcombe, Emma Findlow and Lucien Jenkins for their help and assistance throughout the editing and production process.

Copyright notices

1 Introduction

Madonna has been such a constant presence in our media landscape that it is sometimes difficult to remember that she too was an unknown striving to build a career. Released in 1990 on Sire Records, *The Immaculate Collection* brings together 15 hit songs from the first phase of Madonna's career as a hugely successful pop artist. The album also contains two new songs which went on to be hits and act as pointers to her next phase. Examining the period and the songs from a musical, cultural and historical perspective allows us to trace Madonna's artistic development and to turn a spotlight on the 1980s, a decade which she has come to represent.

The album received some good reviews and was seen as much as a media event as a collection of songs. As journalist James Brown writing in the *New Musical Express* put it, 'The lass Ciccone has long since lost her initial role as a mere singer.' Despite the distraction of Madonna's fame he still came to the conclusion that 'The music's pretty cool.' However because all the tracks had been remixed, the album also drew some negative criticism. The reviewer from music magazine *Record Mirror* summed up the mood: 'The first bars of *Holiday* sound somewhat different to the way you remember them... One thing's for sure: Madonna wasn't sitting on a public toilet when she recorded it, so why does she sound like it now?... though most of the mixes are fine (i.e. barely noticeable), it's still a nasty shock when you're expecting the originals.' Despite the complaints the album went on to sell over 18 million copies.

A guide to various technical terms used in this book can be found on page 61.

The Immaculate Collection

Tracklist	Original album	Year of release	Chart position (US/UK)
1. *Holiday*	*Madonna* (released as *The First Album* outside the USA)	1983	16/6
2. *Lucky Star*	*Madonna*	1983	4/14
3. *Borderline*	*Madonna*	1983	10/2
4. *Like A Virgin*	*Like A Virgin*	1984	1/3
5. *Material Girl*	*Like A Virgin*	1984	2/3
6. *Crazy For You*	*Vision Quest:Original Soundtrack*	1985	2/1

Tracklist	Original album	Year of release	Chart position (US/UK)
7. *Into The Groove*	US B-side to *Angel* maxi-single (rest of the world A-side)	1985	1/1
8. *Live To Tell*	*True Blue*	1986	1/2
9. *Papa Don't Preach*	*True Blue*	1986	1/1
10. *Open Your Heart*	*True Blue*	1986	1/5
11. *La Isla Bonita*	*True Blue*	1986	4/1
12. *Like A Prayer*	*Like A Prayer*	1989	1/1
13. *Express Yourself*	*Like A Prayer*	1989	2/5
14. *Cherish*	*Like A Prayer*	1989	3/2
15. *Vogue*	*I'm Breathless*	1990	1/1 (*Dick Tracy* soundtrack)
16. *Justify My Love**	*The Immaculate Collection*	1990	1/2
17. *Rescue Me**	*The Immaculate Collection*	1990	9/3

*New songs

2

The 1980s: politics, social trends, culture and fashion

Politics

Throughout the 1980s in both the USA and the UK, political power was in the hands of right-wing governments. Republican ex-Hollywood actor Ronald Reagan was President in the White House with Margaret Thatcher Conservative Prime Minister of the British Parliament. They both favoured low tax economies with minimal state intervention in people's affairs. The USA displayed solid economic growth and the country was able to move beyond the traumas of the Vietnam War and Watergate which had so marred the previous decade. This new self-confidence was also displayed in foreign policy. In the second half of the decade and after successful negotiations on nuclear arms reductions, Reagan supported Soviet president Mikhail Gorbachev in the reforms that eventually led to such momentous events as the break up of the Soviet Union, the fall of the Berlin Wall and the reshaping of Eastern Europe.

Politics in the UK was marked by social conflict with polarisation between the political right and left. Under Thatcher's government high unemployment was regarded as a price worth paying for industrial restructuring. Riots expressed political unease with the local government poll tax. Conflicts with the trade unions included the set-piece battles of the miners' strikes. There was also a real war with Argentina over the issue of the sovereignty of the Falkland Islands.

Social trends

The 1980s is often characterised as being a decade dominated by corporate and personal self-interest. Michael Douglas' character Gordon Gecko in the 1986 film *Wall Street* summed up the prevailing mood with his 'greed is good' philosophy. Madonna became known as the 'Material Girl', after the title of one of her biggest hits, and seemed to embody a new spirit that was far away from the anti-materialism of 1970s hippy culture.

Economic conservatism co-existed with a liberalisation of social trends. Women were empowered in business, the professional classes and politics; gay issues came to the fore driven by the AIDS pandemic and the visibility of gay male pop stars; healthy living became big business with an acceptance of the risks of smoking and the growing popularity of jogging, aerobics, vitamin supplements and vegetarianism; racism and other forms of discrimination became less acceptable as 'political correctness' took hold; marriage as an institution was seen to become weaker as 'no fault' divorces and co-habiting rose in popularity.

Popular culture

Popular culture in the 1980s reflected social change. Television audiences enjoyed the conspicuous consumerism of American shows such as *Dallas* and *Dynasty* as well as witnessing the rise of the Afro-American middle-class in *The Cosby Show*. MTV burst onto the scene, changing the way popular music was marketed. Bands were now sold as much on their looks as for their music – and king and queen of this new pop world were Michael Jackson and Madonna. The glamour and fast edits of the pop video were soon reflected in TV shows such as *Miami Vice*. In the UK the more prosaic worlds of soap operas *Brookside* and *Eastenders* took hold on the national consciousness, as did the political satire of puppet show *Spitting Image*.

Fads came and went with *Rubik's Cube, Teenage Mutant Ninja Turtles, Trivial Pursuit* and *Cabbage Patch Dolls* all having a grip on public consciousness. More long-lasting was the emergence of rap, which spawned the hip-hop industry – a classic example of how a localised scene, in this instance in the South Bronx (a predominantly Afro-American neighbourhood in New York City), exploded worldwide in the space of a few years to become a dominant force in popular culture.

Blockbuster movie franchises such as *Terminator, Alien, Die Hard* and *Rambo* were also a prominent feature of the decade. On smaller screens arcade games such as *Space Invaders* became immensely popular and, as PCs and games consoles came onto the market, so did *Pac Man* and *Super Mario Bros*.

Fashion

Excess was the name of the game with big hair and shoulder-padded power suits for career women, while 'New Romantic' men borrowed their sister's eyeliner. Bands influenced hairstyles: asymmetric cuts came in with The Human League while for some, Bruce Springsteen in his jeans and tee-shirt was a more acceptable role model. On the back of the aerobics craze legwarmers were an indispensable fashion item, as were acid-washed jeans and parachute pants.

With the release of her second album *Like A Virgin*, Madonna became the definitive fashion icon for girls. Her look combined short skirts worn over Capri pants, lace tops, beads, fishnet tights, a fake facial mole and most controversially the Christian cross and 'Boy Toy' belt. As well as gaining her many column inches, Madonna's style combined with her music and videos to create an offer to the public that was irresistible.

Questions for further study

Were the social and political changes that took place in the 1980s in any way reflected in Madonna's music and presentation of herself as an artist? Consider the use of new technology, a move away from the values of the 1970s, and the liberalisation of social values.

3

Madonna: early life and career

Detroit was famous as the home of Motown Records. Motown dominated the American pop charts in the 1960s with its synthesis of rhythm and blues, dance music and pop. It was the first label owned by an Afro-American (Berry Gordy) to achieve national and international success. The label featured Afro-American artists such as Diana Ross and The Supremes, Marvin Gaye and Stevie Wonder.

Madonna Louise Ciccone was born in 1958, the third child of a Catholic family in Bay City, Michigan, USA, an industrial town on the banks of Lake Huron. She grew up in the suburbs of nearby Detroit where her Italian-American father Silvio 'Tony' Ciccone worked in the car industry. Her mother, also named Madonna, died in 1963 when her daughter was five and Silvio went on to marry the family's housekeeper.

Madonna was a student at Rochester Adams High School where she achieved good grades and a place in the cheerleading squad. She studied ballet and it was her ballet teacher who, in the mid-1970s, introduced her to the underground gay disco scene, an influence that remains to this day. After high school Madonna studied dance at the University of Michigan for one year before heading off to New York to find work.

In New York she worked with the Alvin Ailey contemporary dance group and in 1979 danced on a tour for French disco artist Patrick Hernandez. Now Madonna was moving in the world of musicians she formed a rock band, *The Breakfast Club*, in which she played guitar, drums and sang. In 1980 she began a musical collaboration with drummer and ex-boyfriend Stephen Bray. Their demos came into the hands of the head of Sire Records, Seymour Stein, who signed Madonna to the label in 1982. Several singles were released and became hits in the US dance charts, encouraging Sire to finance the 1983 release of her debut album entitled *Madonna*.

The three hit singles from *Madonna* established her as an artist who was not just a club favourite, but someone who could have mainstream success in the Billboard Hot 100 pop charts. Madonna also showed that she wanted to exert control over her career by bringing in her boyfriend John 'Jellybean' Benitez to remix the album, as she was unhappy with the sound achieved by original producer Reggie Lucas. The release of the 1984 album *Like A Virgin* saw Madonna move to the forefront of the pop world. She achieved her first US number one with the title track and shot to global fame after appearing at the first MTV Video Music Awards.

Madonna moved into film acting in 1985 with a cameo appearance in *Vision Quest* followed by a starring role in *Desperately Seeking Susan* in which she gained good reviews for playing a character that was not too far removed from her own. The films also acted as vehicles for her recordings, each having its own hit single. Despite this success, music was still the key element in Madonna's career. Her 1986 album *True Blue* consolidated Madonna's position as the top female pop artist in the world and was also seen as an artistic progression with a wider emotional and stylistic range than the two previous albums. The videos for the five hit singles taken from *True Blue* showed more ambition in the production values and a greater thematic sophistication, allowing Madonna to play with issues such as gender, religion and sexuality.

1987 saw Madonna appearing in the film *Who's That Girl?*. Despite the film's failure at the box office, the soundtrack album was still a success, generating two top five singles. The tour that followed was more theatrical in presentation than before and attracted the censure of the Pope, who advised audiences in Italy to boycott it.

The 1989 album *Like A Prayer* also gained good reviews. *Rolling Stone* magazine said the record was 'as close to art as pop music gets'. *Like A Prayer* gave Madonna a further five hits as well as creating controversy over the religious imagery used in the title track's video. Her next film role was more of a success. Madonna was well qualified to play the role of vamp Breathless Mahoney in Warren Beatty's 1990 film *Dick Tracy*. The *I'm Breathless* album contained songs from the film and also a non-film track *Vogue* which became an international hit. The *Blonde Ambition* tour followed and its fusion of religious and sexual imagery combined with showstopping production values raised the bar for touring pop artists, as well as guaranteeing controversy.

The Immaculate Collection was released at the end of 1990 as Madonna's first 'best of' compilation. It received mixed reviews with unhappiness over the album mixes not being those of the original single releases. It was still a great commercial success marking the end of the first phase of Madonna's career, in a decade when her sales were matched only by Michael Jackson. For someone who had started the decade as an unemployed dancer and finished it as one of the *Ladies Home Journal*'s 'Fifty Most Powerful Women In The USA', it was an extraordinary journey.

Questions for further study

What similarities and differences can be found between Madonna's recorded output and that of the Motown label? Consider commercial appeal, target audience, lyrical content and compositional devices such as hooks and typical forms.

4
Technological developments

In the 15 years from 1975 to 1990 there was a huge step forward in the technologies and media that we take for granted today. Personal computing, communications and the entertainment industries were at the forefront of these changes. Within popular music production a transition took place from using electronic equipment with primarily analogue circuitry and a tape-based recording medium, to the digital recording software and hardware that we use today. Here is a timeline that shows when the technologies that were used in the recordings that make up *The Immaculate Collection* were developed.

Technology timeline

1975	New England Digital's Synclavier System, an early digital synthesiser and sampler, is marketed as a 'tapeless studio'. Its price of around $300,000 positioned it at the top end of the market. The facilities it offered (recording, editing, playback and data storage of audio and MIDI information), radical at the time, are now achievable with a PC-based set up costing less than £1,000.
1976	Moog's Polymoog, the Yamaha CS-80 and the Oberheim Four-Voice are the first polyphonic music synthesisers on the market, only affordable for major artists and studios.
1977	Roland launches their first analogue sequencer, the 12-step System 700 modular synthesiser.
1978	Philips brings out the compact disk format. Ry Cooder's album *Bop Till You Drop* is the first completely digitally recorded album in popular music. The influential Sequential Circuits Prophet-5 synthesiser is introduced, the first polyphonic synthesiser to allow multiple patch settings to be saved to a computer microprocessor.
1979	Solid State Logic releases the SSL SL 4000E Master Studio System mixing console featuring compressors and noise gates on every channel, as well as the Total Recall system. This allowed mix setups to be recalled not only on the original mix desk but on any E series in the world. In less than three years, every major studio worldwide featured at least one room with an SSL E Series console.
1980	The Linn LM-1 Drum Computer (priced at $4,999) is the first drum machine to use digital samples. Its sound is one of the defining characteristics of 80s pop. It can be heard on many of Madonna's early tracks. The Roland TR-808 and its successor, TR-909 (1983) are launched as low-cost analogue alternatives to the Linn. It was later in the 1980s that these machines became hugely fashionable in their own right as production tools in the house, techno and hip-hop genres.

1981	MTV is launched in the USA. The first music video shown was *Video Killed the Radio Star* by Buggles. Dave Smith (Sequential Circuits), Ikutaro Kakehashi (Roland) and Tom Oberheim (Oberheim) meet at the June NAMM (National Association of Music Merchants) conference to develop a standard protocol allowing digital musical instruments to communicate. Smith then creates the USI (Universal Synthesiser Interface) protocol, a forerunner of MIDI.
1982	The Fairlight CMI (Computer Music Instrument) Series II becomes the first digital sampler on the market. It also featured an onboard sequencer and later added MIDI and SMPTE functionality. Sequential Circuits launches the Prophet 600, the first MIDI synthesiser.
1983	Yamaha releases the DX-7, the first mass-market synthesiser to utilise FM technology. It combined easy accessibility to huge sound libraries with a clean, fresh digital sound to become the dominant synthesiser of its time. At this year's NAMM, MIDI is born. A Prophet 600 is connected to and controls a Roland JP5.
1984	Sony introduces the first portable CD player.
1985	Paul Hardcastle releases *19*, a worldwide hit with an anti-war message that features and highlights the use of a sampler.
1986	DAT (digital audio tape) two-track stereo tapes and players are launched. Akai brings out the S900, the first affordable digital sampler to become an industry standard.
1987	Akai releases the MPC60 digital sampler/drum machine and MIDI sequencer, a sampler with touch sensitive trigger pads. The MPC series of sampler/sequencers go on to play a crucial role in the emerging rap/hip-hop industries, with their signature swing groove becoming a feature of drum patterns within these genres. Roland launches the D50 synthesiser featuring onboard reverb and chorus effects, and a joystick for data manipulation. The D50 uses a method of sound production known as Linear Arithmetic (LA) synthesis that combines sample playback with digital synthesis.
1988	CD sales pass those of LPs.
1990	Madonna's *The Immaculate Collection* is released, the first album to feature the digital Qsound system for 3D Positional Audio production.

5

Women in popular music

Madonna's musical heroes when growing up in the 1960s were singers such as Motown star Diana Ross, and Ronnie Spector, lead singer of The Ronettes. In the 1970s there were many successful female performers combining talent with originality and style: the intense singer-songwriter Joni Mitchell, the ethereal Kate Bush, and two who particularly influenced the young Madonna, Chrissie Hynde from the Pretenders and Debbie Harry of Blondie. As a young dancer Madonna was exposed to the disco of Gloria Gaynor's *I Will Survive* as well as Donna Summer's *Love To Love You Baby*. It is Summer's euro-disco music of the mid 1970s, produced by Italian producer Giorgio Moroder in the Hansa studios in Berlin, that with its gay appeal and sexual content is the template for much of Madonna's dance music.

As she started her career, Madonna's rivals in the pop market place were singers such as Cyndi Lauper and Debbie Gibson. Lauper in particular struck a chord with audiences. Her 1984 debut album *She's So Unusual* had four top five singles including *Girls Just Want To Have Fun* and *True Colours* and sold in excess of ten million copies. However neither Lauper nor Gibson were able to keep pace with Madonna as the decade unfolded.

Madonna and feminism

In an article in the *New York Times* in 1990, critic Camille Paglia announced to the world that 'Madonna is the future of feminism'. As well as being a hugely successful recording star and fashion template for generations of young women, Madonna holds a unique place in contemporary feminist thought. She combined sexual precocity and independence, personal assertiveness and confidence in business, an ability to play with gender and sexual stereotypes, and took inspiration from the image of female icons such as Marilyn Monroe and Marlene Dietrich. This presents academics with much material to deconstruct and debate. Madonna's empowerment creates a new kind of feminism where women can be glamorous and sexual as well as being strong and independent.

The feminism of the 1970s, as exemplified by writers such as Andrea Dworkin, was a rather dour philosophy in which all heterosexual sexual relationships were viewed as 'rape' and dressing up was a heinous crime. Many young women in the 1980s responded to Madonna's offer that it was possible to dress up and have fun and still be a success in your own right.

Religion and sex

'Crucifixes are sexy because there's a naked man on them.' (Madonna)

The collision of religious iconography such as crucifixes and crosses with sexually provocative visuals and choreography in Madonna's work had roots in her own experience. With a devout Catholic family background and a willingness to confront conservative middle America, she uses her own erotic response to religion to create music and video that are both controversial and commercial.

Madonna's breakthrough hit in the UK was *Like A Virgin*. The song's title combined with Madonna's own name was enough to attract criticism from the church. In the video she dances in a sexual manner – either in her trademark early 80s style accessorised with crosses and rosaries, or in a flouncy white wedding dress.

This look was put together for Madonna by French stylist Maripol and a *Madonna* branded line of accessories and jewellery was marketed to the huge market of 'wannabes' that soon developed across the globe.

In *Like A Prayer* she brings together quasi-spiritual lyrics and the sound of an Afro-American gospel choir with provocative religious visuals such as a burning cross and a black Jesus whom she embraces. Entwined into all of this is the story of a Ku Klux Klan-style lynching with Madonna as witness. Pepsi had paid Madonna five million dollars to use the song in an advert but the company dropped it after coming under pressure from conservative lobby group the American Family Association. Madonna kept the money, the track was a UK/US number one, and again she proved that her cocktail of dance music, religion and sex was an irresistible commercial proposition.

6
Introducing The Immaculate Collection

Marketing

'She's so smart. By the second or third record, she didn't need anybody.' (Sire Records co-founder Seymour Stein)

The process of packaging and marketing a 'best of' collection is only marginally different to putting together an album of new material. Songs, the tracklist and an album title have to be chosen, artwork and photographs commissioned and designed, singles have to be selected and a promotional strategy for the singles and album constructed. For all of the above to fit into a coherent marketing strategy, the separate elements must work with Madonna's marketing USP (unique selling point) – her ability to shock and thereby get attention from the socially conservative elements in American society.

Content

The Immaculate Collection features 15 songs that had been hits for Madonna between1983 and 1990 as well as two new songs, *Justify My Love* and *Rescue Me*.

> Several other hits from the same period such as *Angel, Dress You Up, True Blue, Who's That Girl* and *Causing a Commotion* are missing, to allow space for new songs to be marketed as singles.

In an unusual and controversial move, all of the older songs were remixed by album coordinator Shep Pettibone. The versions of the songs on the album are therefore different to those released as the original singles, creating some annoyance among fans, critics and the original producers alike. Additionally all the songs are processed with a shortlived new technology called Qsound which adds a three-dimensional aspect to stereo sound.

Title and tracklist

The Immaculate Collection was originally titled *The Ultimate Collection*, but this was dropped for the more controversial version. The title plays on the Catholic dogma of the immaculate conception and was a choice guaranteed to gain publicity.

According to a UK pre-release promotional press folder, the tracklist was originally quite different to the one on the album as released, opening with *Like A Virgin*, *Material Girl* and *Crazy For You*, and ending with one new (as yet untitled) song.

The final decision to position the songs chronologically serves to create a focus on the two new songs presented at the end of the album.

Artwork and photographs

As with her previous albums *The Immaculate Collection* was set to feature a cover photo of Madonna. In this instance a black and white shot was chosen, taken by Herb Ritts of Madonna in a men's toilet. However, Madonna decided that the picture made her look 'too much like Mike Tyson' (a heavyweight boxing champion). The mock heraldic logo, designed by Jeri and John Heiden to frame the album title, ended up being used for the whole cover with the Ritts shots being featured throughout the booklet.

Music promotion and MTV

The US video channel MTV started broadcasting in 1981 just as Madonna was beginning her career. Its 24/7 output created a demand for new artists who were young, good-looking and visually aware. Groups such as Duran Duran and Culture Club came from the UK, setting off what is sometimes referred to as the second British invasion (the first being that spearheaded by groups such as the Beatles, the Rolling Stones and the Dave Clark Five in the early 1960s). By the mid-1980s, getting videos onto the MTV playlist had become crucial to the success of any new artist and many older musicians struggled to adapt to the new medium.

From the success of *Like A Virgin* onwards Madonna was the embodiment of an MTV artist. Edgy and controversial enough to attract the youth market, but capable of creating a steady stream of hit songs, she dominated the MTV awards and set the tone for the channel. However, the sexual content of the Jean-Baptiste Mondino-directed video for *Justify My Love*, the first single from *The Immaculate Collection*, proved to be too much of a risk for MTV bosses. The video was banned and the subsequent publicity helped to create the biggest-selling video single ever. *The Immaculate Collection* was propelled to international sales of over 18 million copies.

7

Track-by-track analysis

In this chapter you will find full analyses of two songs, *Holiday* and *Vogue*, as well as short-form analyses of all the other songs on *The Immaculate Collection*.

Holiday

Duration	4'00"
BPM/time signature	118/$\frac{4}{4}$
Composer(s)	Curtis Hudson/Lisa Stevens
Original album	*Madonna*
Producer(s)	John 'Jellybean' Benitez
Remixed for *The Immaculate Collection* by	Shep Pettibone and Goh Hotoda
Instrumentation/musician credits	Drums, Moog bass, OB-X synthesiser, Fender Rhodes, acoustic piano: Fred Zarr
	Guitars: Curtis Hudson
	Bass: Raymond Hudson
	Percussion: Bashiri Johnson
	Cowbell: Madonna
	Backing vocals: Madonna, Tina B, Norma Jean Wright

Song history

John 'Jellybean' Benitez was brought in to do some remixing on the *Madonna* album as Madonna felt producer Reggie Lucas' work was 'overarranged'. At that point Benitez suggested recording *Holiday*. Released as the third single from Madonna, it was Madonna's first record to cross over into the Billboard Hot 100, reaching number 16. *Holiday* helped re-establish dance music in the mainstream American pop charts. At 4'00", the remixed version on *The Immaculate Collection* is considerably shorter than the 6'08" version on *Madonna*.

Song section	Bars (length)	Position in song
Introduction	16	0′00″
'Holiday' chant 1	8	0′33″
Chorus 1	8	0′49″
Verse 1	8	1′05″
Bridge 1	8	1′22″
Chorus 2	8	1′38″
Instrumental breakdown 1	8	1′55″
Verse 2	8	2′11″
Bridge 2	8	2′27″
Chorus 3	8	2′44″
Instrumental breakdown 2	8	3′00″
'Holiday' chant 2	8	3′16″
Chorus 4	8	3′33″
'Holiday' chant 3 (to fade)	8	3′49″

Song analysis

Key: D major

The song opens with a four-bar 'pad' chord sequence (|G to A|A to Bm|G to A|F♯m to G|):

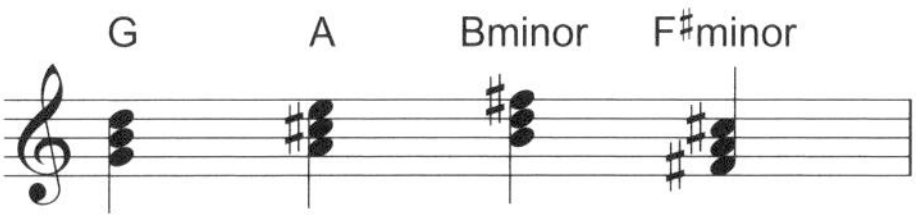

This is played on a Fender Rhodes electric piano accompanied by some busy percussion (bongos, cowbells and tambourine):

This groove acts as the basis for the whole song. Synthesised strings enter on beat 4 of bar 4 of the **Introduction** with a pick-up that leads into a melodic hook. This takes us through to a B minor (chord VI) synthesiser stab on beat 4 of bar 8. The stab is preceded by a beat of reverse reverb on the programmed handclaps and is also marked by the drums. The next four bars repeat the four-bar sequence with the addition of a funky synthesiser bass line:

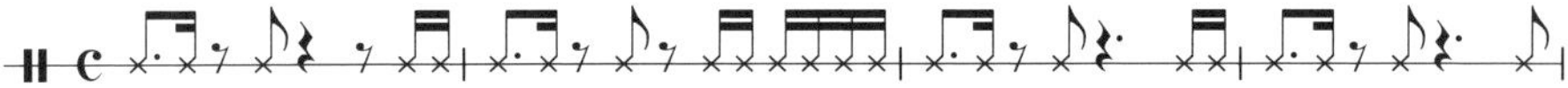

This plays against the classic disco four-to-the-floor-style drums. Bars 13–16 feature the addition of a Chic-style rhythm guitar pattern:

Chic were the most critically acclaimed Disco group of the late 1970s.

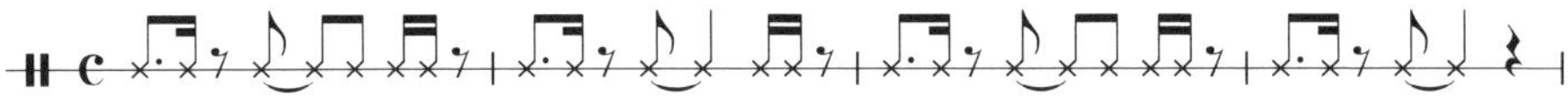

This follows the chord sequence while adding further rhythmic impetus. On the top is a two-bar analogue synthesiser melody (the OB-X) played in 3rds and 4ths that not only starts on the same beat of the bar, but also shares the first three notes of the earlier string line. Two short hi-hat fills then lead us into the **'Holiday' chant 1**, a unison, multi-voice, two-note chant based on the words 'holiday' and 'celebrate'. This chant repeats twice over an eight-bar section and is perfect for dancers to sing along to. The rhythm section groove adds its final element in this section with a funky, syncopated electric guitar part.

After the chant comes **Chorus 1**, a simply sung syllabic and diatonic melody. It starts with a pick-up on beat 4 of the previous section and then builds to the end of the eight-bar section with a vocal harmony overdub on the last line ('It would be so nice'). The first line of the first four-bar chorus section is answered by a repeating three-note ascending synthesiser motif, the first line of the second section by a lush synthesised string pad. Madonna's vocal tone is very clear, ranging from a light-sounding chest tone to a more focused nasal tone as she enters the upper registers. When harmony backing vocals enter (as opposed to the unisons that happened earlier) they are built on the chord tones around the melody, normally one above and one below. The backing vocalists match their timbres to Madonna's.

Verse 1 and **Bridge 1** stick to the same type of pentatonic melodic patterns as the chorus and double-track the lead vocal at the end of every eight bars for added emphasis ('We need a holiday'). On the first four bars of **Bridge 1** a two-note string countermelody helps to build tension as the vocal rises in pitch and intensity. **Chorus 2** features a highly reverberated vocal ad-lib and is followed by the first **Instrumental breakdown.** This features all the rhythm section instruments minus the Fender Rhodes and there is a question-and-answer dialogue between the synthesiser part from the introduction (the first five notes with a minim repeat delay) and the picked rhythm guitar.

Verse 2 and **Bridge 2** are reruns of the first verse and bridge, followed by **Chorus 3** which adds more substantial unison backing vocals than before. **Instrumental breakdown 2** again drops the Rhodes but this time features a new two-bar repeated synthesiser line, which reverses the melodic shape of the one from the introduction. This adds to the sense of repetition, which is necessary for dance music, although the changes, albeit small, create variety.

The 'Holiday' chant 2 section (this time with the minim delay used earlier on the synthesiser) is just accompanied by the drums and percussion (including a timbale solo) and is followed by **Chorus 4** with added reverbed ad-libs. The full backing track and vocal ad-libs of the **'Holiday' Chant 3** section fade quickly to end the song.

Comparing versions

The version of *Holiday* on *The Immaculate Collection* doesn't have the raw energy of the original from the *Madonna* album. The Benitez version is clearly aimed at the dancefloor; its introduction just features the Rhodes, bass drum and tambourine, making it easy for DJs to mix into from other tracks. It is considerably longer at 6'08" with doubled choruses, extra vocal ad-lib sections and a piano solo at the end.

From a sonic perspective it is a classic piece of early 1980s dance pop. The synthesisers and drums are positioned in the forefront of the mix and reverbs are used as effects rather than trying to create a naturalistic soundfield. The Shep Pettibone remix is smoother and the rhythm section is more fully integrated with the vocals. The track sounds as if it has been vari-sped to make it slightly faster and sharper and the song structure is more typical of a pop radio mix.

Variable speed pitch control (vari-speed) is a control on an audio device that allows the operator to deviate from a standard speed, and if done using tape also changes the pitch.

Vogue

Duration	5'17"
BPM/time signature	116/$\frac{4}{4}$
Composer(s)	Madonna/Shep Pettibone
Original album	*I'm Breathless*
Producer(s)	Madonna/Shep Pettibone
Remixed for *The Immaculate Collection* by	Shep Pettibone and Goh Hotoda
Instrumentation/musician credits	Programming: Alan Friedman
	Background vocals: Niki Haris, Donna DeLory and Ndea Davenport

Song history

Composed by Madonna and Shep Pettibone, *Vogue* was based on the dance of the same name popular in New York gay and transvestite clubs. Dancers would 'strike a pose' imitating the look of models on the covers of high-fashion magazines, as well as making angular hand and arm movements that were associated with particular female Hollywood icons. The track was originally intended to be a B-side to *Keep It Together* (from the *Like A Prayer* album), but executives at Warner Brothers convinced Madonna that it should be an A-side in its own right. It was released as a single and with its stylish black and white video became a UK/US number one. It was added to the *I'm Breathless* album, the soundtrack to the *Dick Tracy* movie in which Madonna co-starred with her new boyfriend Warren Beatty, and helped promote both the soundtrack and the movie.

Song section	Bars (length)	Position in song
Spoken intro	-	0'00"
Introduction 1	24	0'02"
Introduction 2	16	0'52"
Verse 1	16	1'25"
Chorus 1	8	1'58"
Verse 2	16	2'15"
Chorus 2	8	2'48"
Middle 8	11	3'04"
Chorus 3	8	3'27"
Link	8	3'43"
Rap	16	4'00"
Breakdown	8	4'33"
Chorus 4	8	4'50"
Coda (with spoken ending)	4	5'06"

Song analysis

Key: A♭ major

Vogue opens with the spoken words 'What are you looking at?'. Madonna's delivery is intentionally camp to introduce us into the gay subculture that she celebrates in the song. The vocal pans across from right to left and is quite wet. The track then creeps in (**Introduction 1**) with eight bars of a warm analogue synthesiser pad (E♭m7 to A♭9) and a high, synthetic, two-note string line. The next four bars add reverbed fingerclicks on beats 2 and 4 and then in

'Wet' in audio terms means that the signal has additional reverberation (or reverb) added. 'Dry' means the opposite.

bars 13–16 a bongo beat enters:

This is reminiscent of a shortened 3-2 salsa clave. A house music-style sub-bass sound enters in the final eight bars of this opening introductory section:

Sub-bass is a term used to describe audible sounds below 90Hz.

This sits rhythmically with the first three notes of the bongo part and then creates an offbeat pattern that moves between E♭, G♭ and A♭. The bass notes create harmonic ambivalence. Are we in E♭ minor as the bass implies, or is E♭ actually a dominant waiting to be resolved to its tonic (A♭) which is suggested by the high strings? At this point (**Introduction 2**) the drums enter with a typical house beat featuring a skipping snare drum. Madonna coolly delivers the words 'strike a pose'. This vocal is completely dry and contrasts with the slightly camp delivery and use of reverb in the spoken intro. A rhythmic electric piano chord marks the downbeat of each bar and has a crotchet delay allowing it to bleed into beat two.

In bar 8 of this section the electric piano and snare play a semiquaver fill pattern (a typical Shep Pettibone motif) that moves us forward to the next eight bars.

In this eight-bar section the fingerclicks drop out and are replaced with an agogo bell loop. The loop is mixed quite low in the track and has had its lower frequencies filtered out so that it doesn't interfere sonically with the rest of the track. The bass line and the harmony instruments move to the key of A♭ where they remain for the rest of the track. The strings continue with their two-note motif and a synthesiser harmonises a 4th below. In the mid-range a sampled synthesiser stab has a semiquaver delay (it runs for 1½ beats) and marks the downbeat every two bars. There are also sampled brass stabs, and an offbeat sampled string stab and snare fill lead into the beginning of **Verse 1**.

The downbeat of Verse 1 is emphasised by the use of a sampled orchestral stab (A♭). With that addition, the backing track for the first eight bars of the verse is similar to the previous eight bars, with the stabs being replaced by a double-tracked mixolydian vocal melody. Backing vocals interject, crossing over the lead at times. For the next eight bars the pad, rhythmic electric piano and high strings from the introduction return as the vocal builds in intensity towards **Chorus 1**, assisted by a vocal harmony in 3rds, snare fills and string stabs. The downbeat of Chorus 1 is also marked by an orchestral stab which sets off an insistent house-style riff played on a sampled piano, based on descending minor chords:

This riff is punctuated by quieter orchestral stabs but the mix allows the vocal lead (still double-tracked) to dominate. The simple vocal melody is constructed on A♭, B♭ and C♭ and is answered by a higher backing vocal, again in 3rds. The word 'Vogue' is whispered as a backing vocal, coming in on the downbeat of bars 2 and 6 of the chorus.

Verse 2 and Chorus 1 repeat the format of the first verse and chorus with the addition of an unusual vocal stab in the second chorus using the word 'Vogue' made up of the notes A♭, B♭ and D♭.

The **Middle 8** is an 11-bar section that initially uses the verse backing track with the addition of an organ pad, a new melodic line and supporting backing vocals. At bar 8 it moves from the tonic to the dominant for a four-bar build. The vocal melody gets higher and more intense climaxing with the phrase 'Get up on the dance floor'. The vocal is again supported by a semiquaver snare drum fill and backing vocals, leading into **Chorus 3** which is a repeat of Chorus 2. **Chorus 3** is followed by an eight-bar **Link** section that uses the chorus backing without the piano but with the addition of an offbeat synthesiser part. There is also a spoken vocal ('Beauty's where you find it') that enters on the downbeats of bars 3 and 8 and is mixed quite low in the track.

The **Rap** section is 16 bars long and uses the chorus backing track with the piano riff entering in the second half. The rap itself lists the names of Hollywood screen icons and is pitched low in Madonna's vocal range. There are a couple of moments ('Gene Kelly, Fred Astaire' and 'Rita Hayworth gave good face') where the vocal sound becomes much wetter. It is generally assumed that these lyrics were replacements as the originals were deemed too adult for the Disney-produced film.

It seems there was a lack of care in matching the vocal sound as the dropped-in lyrics sound very obvious.

The **Rap** is followed by an eight-bar **Breakdown** section where all the percussion instruments drop out leaving the chorus piano riff, joined after four bars by the bass. Madonna speaks the word 'Vogue' every two bars and the vocal has a crotchet delay and repeats several times fading into the track. There are also sampled brass stabs and the chorus backing vocals.

Chorus 4 is very much the same as those that preceded it, with the addition of an ad-libbed lead vocal and without the other vocal interjections. It also features an unexpected orchestral stab at the start of bar 3. This use of variety helps hold the listener's interest.

At the end of Chorus 4 the track appears to be continuing along the same lines, but on bar 3 of the **Coda** the orchestral stabs return with four crotchet beats. The track ends with Madonna's voice speaking the title lyric with the crotchet delay fading. Underneath the vocal, the sound of the backing track bleeding through from Madonna's headphones can be heard.

Comparing versions

Shep Pettibone's experience as an innovative dance music producer helped shape this version, with his trademark snare fills, the long introduction, drop-outs and builds – all typical dance-music production techniques of this period. Combined with Madonna's ability to fuse elements from different subcultures and musical styles, the outcome was one of Madonna's most successful records ever.

The original version from the *I'm Breathless* album doesn't have the spoken word opening and condenses the first 24 bars into 16, with the bass entering at the same time as the bongos and fingerclicks. Otherwise the mix and arrangement is much the same.

The following analyses are condensed and focus on the main elements in the recording.

Lucky Star

Duration	3'36"
BPM/time signature	118/$\frac{4}{4}$
Composer(s)	Madonna
Original album	*Madonna*
Producer(s)	Reggie Lucas
	Remixed by John 'Jellybean' Benitez
Remixed for *The Immaculate Collection* by	Shep Pettibone and Goh Hotoda
Instrumentation/musician credits	Synthesisers: Dean Gant, Fred Zarr, Ed Walsh
	Linn Drum programming: Reggie Lucas, Leslie Ming
	Background vocals: Gwen Guthrie, Norma Jean Wright, Madonna, Brenda White, Chrissy Faith

Song history

Lucky Star was the first song to be written by Madonna after signing her record deal and the last single to be released from her first album. It was the first in her series of 16 consecutive American top five hits.

Song section	Bars (length)	Position in song
Arpeggiated synth intro	4	0'00"
Rhythm section introduction 1	8	0'08"
Verse 1	8	24"
Chorus 1	8	40"
Verse 2	8	57"
Chorus 2	8	1'13"
Middle 8	16	1'29"
Verse 3 (low-pitched vocal)	8	2'01"
Chorus 3	8	2'18"
Middle 8	16	2'34"
Verse 4 (ad-lib)	8	3'06"
Chorus 4 (to fade)	8	3'23"

Song analysis

Key: E minor

From its **Arpeggiated synth intro** onwards, *Lucky Star* is a classic slice of 1980s pop/dance. The verse and chorus are built around the same three-chord (E minor, C major and D major), two-bar groove. The synthesised bass and programmed Linn drums provide a solid foundation for the more rhythmic, functional or decorative elements in the rhythm track – such as the analogue synthesiser pad, synthesised brass stabs, synthesised flute (in 4ths), high synthesised bell and the funky picked electric guitar parts. The **Middle 8** sees the addition of a distorted electric guitar and synthesised marimba part to create an even more frenetic mood.

Madonna's vocal is mostly placed in her upper chest register which gives it a punchy aggressive sound. However, in the two-chord middle 8 the vocal is pitched much lower. To add some strength and attitude here, the vocal is double-tracked and Madonna half-speaks a few of the words for added emphasis. The verse/chorus melodies are mostly pitched within the compass of a 5th, using simple melodic patterns. Other sections of the song are also simply constructed making the melody easy to sing. The chorus vocal is built up using backing vocals to differentiate it from the verse.

Production tip: Listen out for electric guitar slides adding emphasis and texture.

Exercise

Notate the first four bars of the synthesised bass part from the rhythm section introduction at 0'08".

Borderline

Duration	3'58"
BPM/time signature	119/$\frac{4}{4}$
Composer(s)	Reggie Lucas
Original album	*Madonna*
Producer(s)	Reggie Lucas
	Remixed by John 'Jellybean' Benitez
Remixed for *The Immaculate Collection* by	Shep Pettibone and Goh Hotoda
Instrumentation/musician credits	Synthesisers: Dean Gant, Fred Zarr, Ed Walsh
	Electric and acoustic pianos: Dean Gant, Fred Zarr
	Electric bass: Anthony Jackson
	Linn Drum programming: Reggie Lucas, Leslie Ming
	Background vocals: Gwen Guthrie, Norma Jean Wright, Madonna, Brenda White, Chrissy Faith.

Song history

Borderline established Madonna as an artist who was striving to be more than just a dance act. Although fairly upbeat, the song's melody and lyrics are more balladic in style than her other early songs and Madonna's delivery has the virtue of sounding sincere. The video for *Borderline* helped to establish Madonna's visual identity and was her first to be heavily rotated on MTV.

Song section	**Bars (length)**	**Position in song**
DX7 Intro	8	0'00"
Rhythm section intro 1	8	0'16"
Verse 1	16	0'32"
Bridge 1	8	1'04"
Chorus 1	16	1'20"
Rhythm section intro 2	8	1'52"

Song section	Bars (length)	Position in song
Verse 2	16	2′08″
Bridge 2	8	2′40″
Chorus 2	16	2′56″
Chorus 3 (ad-lib to fade)	16	3′29″

Song analysis

Key: D major

Borderline's **DX7 Intro** features one of the iconic sounds of 1980s pop productions, the Yamaha DX7 electric piano. A smattering of DX7 bells makes the sound even more bright and sparkling. A drum fill (lo-tom, snare and reverse cymbal) brings in the **Rhythm section intro 1**: a sparse Linn drum groove alongside a funky synthesised bass and programmed cowbell sit underneath a warm analogue lead synthesiser line and an acoustic piano/electric piano pad. As the vocal enters for **Verse 1**, the two-bar, three-chord (D, C and G/B) groove of the introduction continues – minus the lead synth but with the addition of a high, repeated, one-note string line and a percussive synthesiser part.

Bridge 1 has a greater harmonic density, using first and second inversions to good effect. The vocal is set off by gospel-style answering phrases and an ascending synthesiser counter-melody. Synthesised brass stabs lead us into **Chorus 1** and it is here that we find the most unusual feature of the song. The chorus melody enters a minor 3rd lower than the last note of the bridge and its first chord is a dominant first inversion (A/C♯), rather than the tonic that the A chord at the end of the bridge suggests. Both these elements lead to a low-key chorus that needs big backing vocals and synthesised strings and brass to give it some impact.

Madonna's vocal is more ambitious here than in some of her other early recordings; there is a larger compass and some attempt at emotion. The voice has a slapback delay that adds character.

Production tip: Note how the arrangement always creates space for the vocal both in terms of frequencies and parts.

Exercise

On the stave below, fill in the chords for the first eight bars of the chorus from the following:

A, A/C♯, B minor, D/F♯, D/A, E, E minor, E/G♯, F♯/A♯

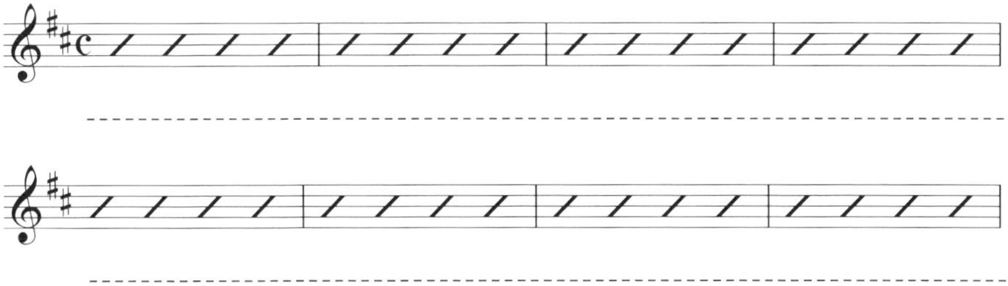

Like A Virgin

Duration	3′10″
BPM/time signature	119/$\frac{4}{4}$
Composer(s)	Billy Steinberg/Tom Kelly
Original album	*Like A Virgin*
Producer(s)	Nile Rodgers
Remixed for *The Immaculate Collection* by	Shep Pettibone and Goh Hotoda
Instrumentation/musician credits	Electric guitar: Nile Rodgers
	Electric bass: Bernard Edwards
	Drums: Tony Thompson
	Assorted synthesisers, bass synthesiser: Rob Sabino

Song history

Madonna's live performance of *Like A Virgin* at the 1984 MTV Video Awards show, complete with white wedding dress and veil, firmly established her in the public's consciousness. The composers' original demo can be heard online at www.songwriteruniverse.com/virgin.html. It provides a fascinating comparison with Madonna's version, produced by Nile Rodgers of Chic, and featuring the band's rhythm section. *Like A Virgin* reached number four in the *Rolling Stone/* MTV list of '100 Greatest Pop Songs'.

Song section	Bars (length)	Position in song
Introduction 1	4	0′00″
Verse 1	8	0′08″
Bridge 1	10	0′24″
Chorus 1	8	0′44″

Song section	Bars (length)	Position in song
Verse 2	8	1′00″
Bridge 2	10	1′17″
Chorus 2	8	1′36″
Middle 8	8	1′52″
Bridge 3	10	2′08″
Chorus 3	8	2′29″
Chorus 4	8	2′45″
Chorus 5 (to fade)	8	3′01″

Song analysis

Key: G♭ major

A three-note, pulsing, synthesised bass line introduces this song, accompanied by sparse hi-hat, bass drum and chunky-sounding synthesiser chords. A snare fill:

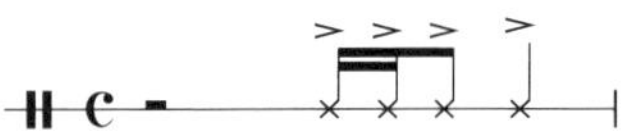

leads into **Verse 1** which continues with a similar feel, the kit keeping a simple beat. Madonna's girlish vocal delivers a major pentatonic melody that continues into the bridge with the addition of synthesised harpsichord interjections. The bridge then begins to build with the bass, now doubled with electric bass, moving to single-pitch quavers. The synthesiser pad loses its rhythmic element, the drums build and the vocal is double-tracked ('Shiny and new').

Chorus 1 is preceded by an ascending synthesiser glissando and snare hit that lead us back into the verse feel, with the addition of synthesised bells and a funky picked electric guitar part. The chorus vocal is also double-tracked and is harmonically ambivalent. The **Middle 8** shifts to the relative minor with a two-chord vamp (E♭ minor to A♭) with heavy synthesiser pads and descending synthesiser arpeggios.

> **Production tip:** Listen to how the drum fills and cymbal crashes often come in unexpected places, adding energy to the track.

Exercise

Add pitches below to the first bar of synthesised bass. Choose from G♭, E♭ and D♭.

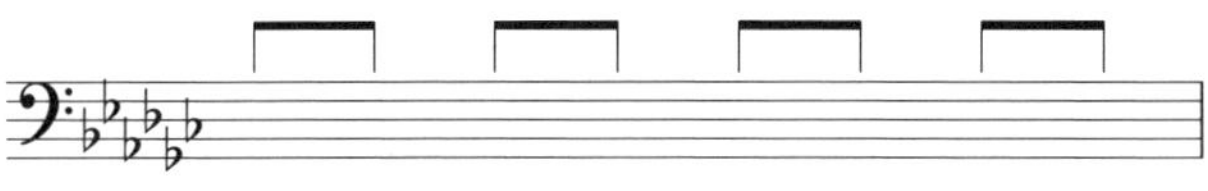

Material Girl

Duration	3'50"
BPM/time signature	134/$\frac{4}{4}$
Composer(s)	Peter Brown/Robert Rans
Original album	*Like A Virgin*
Producer(s)	Nile Rodgers
Remixed for *The Immaculate Collection* by	Shep Pettibone and Michael Hutchinson
Instrumentation/musician credits	Electric guitar, Synclavier II, Roland Juno 60 synthesiser: Nile Rodgers
	Electric bass: Bernard Edwards
	Drums: Tony Thompson
	Background vocals: Madonna, Curtis King, Frank Simms, George Simms.

Song history

After the success of *Like A Virgin,* the release of *Material Girl* cemented Madonna's persona with the public as she became known by the song's title. Madonna is quoted as saying that she would rather not have recorded the song if she had known that its title would become her nickname.

Song section	**Bars (length)**	**Position in song**
Introduction 1	16	0'00"
Verse 1	16	0'29"
Chorus 1	7	0'58"
Introduction 2	4	1'10"
Verse 2	16	1'17"
Chorus 2	7	1'46"
Introduction 3	8	1'58"
Verse 3 (half b/vox, half lead)	16	2'13"
Chorus 3	8	2'41"
Chorus 4	7	2'56"
Introduction 4	3	3'08"
Vocal breakdown	4	3'13"

Song section	Bars (length)	Position in song
Verse 4 (half b/vox and ad-libs, half b/vox drums dropout)	16	3'21"

Song analysis

Key: C major

Opening with a sparse drum fill from drummer Tony Thompson, *Material Girl* sets off with a jaunty two-note synthesiser bass line and Thompson's drum groove augmented by the occasional reverbed clap. An analogue synthesiser enters with a simple repetitive riff and is soon followed by an offbeat synthesised bell and a two-bar synthesised electric guitar line that is repeated an octave above.

Verse 1 continues the groove, going through an eight-bar chord pattern that repeats. The vocal gradually climbs up from the tonic (C) to the flattened 7th (B♭) using the mixolydian scale and supported by low-male backing vocals, as well as Madonna's own ad-libs. Another fill brings in the seven-bar **Chorus 1** which moves between chords F, G and A minor. Madonna's vocal starts back down on the tonic rising only to a G, but the chorus is lifted by higher backing vocals and an arpeggiated, chorused guitar part that rises up an octave for its second half.

Other interesting points include Madonna's signature yelping sounds in later **Introduction** sections and the **Vocal breakdown** section.

Production tip: Nile Rodgers creates interest in the song by reusing old elements in new ways, using a Synclavier synthesiser.

Exercise

The chords in the verse are as follows. C, D minor, G, A minor, B♭. Assign them to their correct positions below.

Crazy For You

Duration	3'44"
BPM/time signature	96/$\frac{4}{4}$
Composer(s)	John Bettis/Jon Lind
Original album	*Vision Quest: Original Soundtrack*
Producer/s	John 'Jellybean' Benitez
Remixed for *The Immaculate Collection* by	Shep Pettibone and Michael Hutchinson
Instrumentation/musician credits	Arrangement: Rob Mounsey
	Drums: Stephen Bray
	Synthesiser strings (Roland Jupiter8 and 2 DX7s MIDIed together): Rob Mounsey
	Synthesisers: Rob Mounsey
	Oboe: George Marge

Song history

Madonna was not initially keen on this song for the soundtrack of a film called *Vision Quest*. The idea to feature an oboe on the track was Madonna's. Arranger Rob Mounsey quotes her as saying: 'You know how in movies there's always an oboe? Let's do that.' Her instincts were good and the song was Madonna's second American number one.

Song section	Bars (length)	Position in song
Introduction 1	8½	0'00"
Verse 1	16	0'22"
Chorus 1	8	1'03"
Introduction 2	5½	1'23"
Verse 2	16	1'34"
Chorus 2	16	2'15"
Introduction 3	8	2'55"
Chorus 3 (ad-lib to fade)	12	3'16"

Song analysis

Key: E major

Despite its slower tempo, *Crazy For You* is immediately recognisable as a Madonna track. Introduced by Stephen Bray's three-quaver drum fill, the song opens with a repeated I, IV, V chord sequence (E, A and B) with movement being supplied by a programmed and synthesised marimba part. The drums and synthesiser bass are fairly static at this point with colour being added by an analogue synthesiser brass line in the middle of the track, synthesised Bell Rhodes flourishes, a synthesised distorted guitar part in 3rds (two DX7s each playing through an Ibanez Tube Screamer stomp box), cymbal rolls and an elegiac oboe line. This feel continues into the first half of **Verse 1**, with the second half being lifted by an arpeggiated DX7 Koto line and the synthesiser brass counter-melody up an octave. Madonna's vocal starts low in her range (G♯) and reaches a high B in the chorus – this wide compass allows her to give an emotional vocal performance. The reverberation added to her voice allows it to dominate the track, making up for some of her vocal shortcomings.

> A Bell Rhodes is a synthesised Fender Rhodes electric piano synthesiser patch, popular in the 1980s, with a bell-like timbre.

The **Chorus 1** vocal is double-tracked and supported by Madonna's own backing vocals. By this point the drums are playing a fuller beat and the synthesiser bass has moved to a semiquaver feel to help propel the track along. **Chorus 3** has the addition of an additional ad-lib vocal hook which adds energy to the end of the song.

> **Production tip:** The snare drum level is unnaturally high (a feature of 80s power ballads) adding weight to the track without any other instruments having to compete with the vocals.

Exercise

Transcribe the Chorus 1 melody using the rhythms provided below.

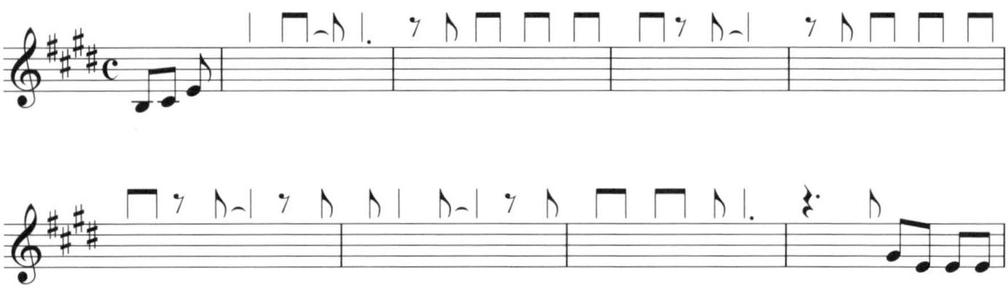

Into the Groove

Duration	4'07"
BPM/time signature	118/$\frac{4}{4}$
Composer(s)	Madonna/Stephen Bray
Original album	US B-side to *Angel* maxi-single. Rest of the world A-side.
Producer/s	Madonna/Stephen Bray
	Additional production by Shep Pettibone
Remixed for *The Immaculate Collection* by	Shep Pettibone and Goh Hotoda
Instrumentation/musician credits	Programming: Stephen Bray

Song history

Into The Groove re-established Madonna's position as a dance music artist, reaching number one in the US dance charts. It featured in the film *Desperately Seeking Susan*, a comedy in which Madonna co-starred with Rosanna Arquette. Madonna's character in the film was similar to her public persona and was another factor in establishing the Madonna 'brand'.

Song section	Bars (length)	Position in song
Introduction 1	8	0'00"
Chorus 1	8	0'16"
Verse 1	16	0'33"
Chorus 2	8	1'06"
Verse 2	16	1'22"
Chorus 3	8	1'55"
Middle 8: 1	8	2'12"
Piano solo	16	2'28"
Middle 8: 2	8	3'01"
Chorus 4	8	3'17"
Chorus 5 (alternate vocal)	8	3'34"
Chorus 6 (to fade)	8	3'50"

Song analysis

Key: C minor

Backed by synthesiser chords and some infectious Latin percussion (cabasa to the right and agogos to the left of the stereo), *Into The Groove* sets off with Madonna's spoken vocal (with a crotchet delay and several repeats) calling dancers out onto the dancefloor. Rising synthesiser bells and a classic 80s-sounding programmed snare/clap fill lead into **Chorus 1**. Madonna's double-tracked vocal is at its most nasal and bubblegum here as the rhythm section pounds away. A mechanistic synthesiser bass line drives the track alongside the more basic drum and busy percussion tracks. The synthesiser chords and bells continue to articulate the harmony, a repetitive four-bar sequence built from the chords C minor, A♭ and B♭. The chorus melody is constructed solely from the notes of the C minor 7th chord (C, E♭, G and B♭).

The energy level diminishes slightly as **Verse 1** enters (a two-bar Cminor, G minor, F minor, G minor sequence) with a simpler bass line and a vocal that skips around between low C and high D.

The **Middle 8** is again constructed on a two-bar sequence, this time a bar of G to a bar of F, and features Madonna harmonising with herself in 3rds. It leads into a lengthy house-style piano solo which uses the C blues scale over the chorus chords. **Chorus 5** features an alternate chorus melody again in 3rds.

Production tip: Ebbs and flows of energy can be created in a track by having a greater and then lesser density of notes in a rhythm part.

Exercise

Transcribe the first four bars of the Chorus 1 melody.

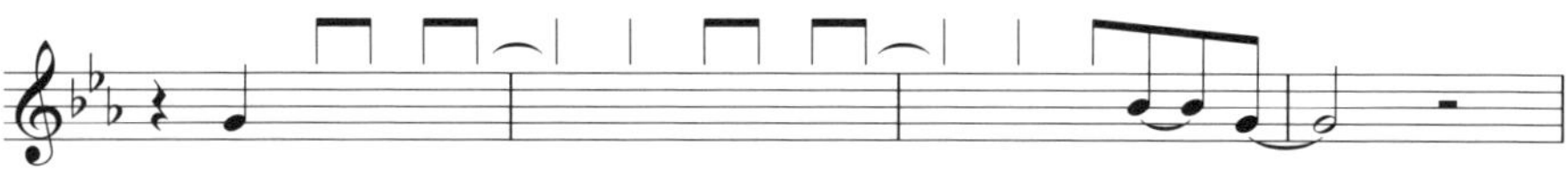

Live to Tell

Duration	5'15"
BPM/time signature	109/$\frac{4}{4}$
Composer(s)	Madonna/Patrick Leonard
Original album	*True Blue*
Producer(s)	Madonna/Patrick Leonard
Remixed for *The Immaculate Collection* by	Shep Pettibone and Michael Hutchinson
Instrumentation/musician credits	Drums: Jonathan Moffett
	Drum programming: Patrick Leonard
	Keyboards: Patrick Leonard
	Guitars: Bruce Gaitsch
	Background vocals: Madonna

Song history

Written for husband Sean Penn's film *At Close Range, Live To Tell* addresses the theme of child abuse and was Madonna's second hit ballad. It received good reviews for its serious subject matter and Madonna's attempt at a more adult-sounding vocal.

Song section	**Bars (length)**	**Position in song**
Out of time introduction	n/a	0'00"
Rhythm section introduction 1	8	0'19"
Verse 1	16	0'36"
Chorus 1	9	1'11"
Rhythm section introduction 2	8	1'32"
Verse 2	16	1'49"
Chorus 2	11	2'23"
Chorus 3	9	2'47"
Out of time link	n/a	3'07"
Middle 8	16	3'37"
Instrumental link	4	4'11"
Chorus 4	11	4'20"

Song section	Bars (length)	Position in song
Chorus 5	11	4'44"
Chorus 6 (to fade)	11	5'08"

Song analysis

Key: F major

Live to Tell opens with a low synthesiser drone over which an electric piano/pad sound plays a series of out-of-time 4ths and 5ths, building up a sustained D minor 11 chord. The rhythm section then bring in **Introduction 1** which consists of four bars repeated – two bars of the D minor 11 chord followed by a four-chord movement (F/A, B♭, F major 7/C, B♭). Reverse reverbs are used quite effectively to provide dramatic textural effects in this introduction, which presents Madonna in 'serious' mode.

Verse 1 uses a repeated four-bar sequence using chords C and G minor 7. Madonna's vocal is in the softer mid-region of her voice and careful use of reverberation makes her voice the focal point of the track. As the song moves into the chorus the vocal goes down as far as a low F, although the meandering, pensive melody then moves as far as the octave above. **Chorus 1** shifts between chords F, A minor, B♭, C and D minor. Momentum is added by an arpeggiated pizzicato-style synthesiser part and Madonna's vocal is heavily compressed.

Verse 2 adds a rhythm guitar part and **Chorus 2** brings in synthesiser strings that build through **Chorus 3.** The **Middle 8** sees the addition of a vocal counter-melody/harmony with a second reappearing on the outgoing choruses.

Production tip: Heavy compression on a vocal allows softer vocals to be audible, as the compression brings down the level of louder sections allowing the whole vocal to be turned up.

Exercise

Using the pitches C, D F and G transcribe the semiquaver synthesiser part at 0'23" for 2 bars.

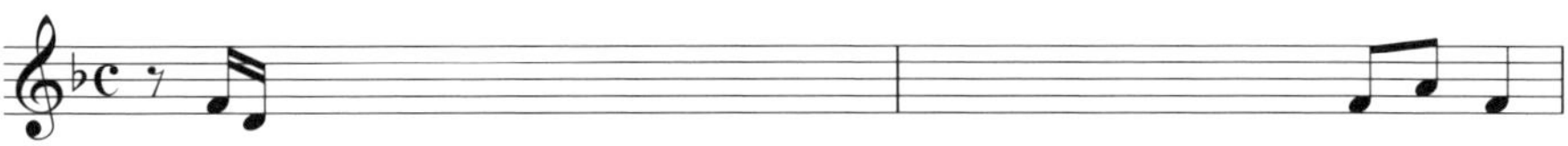

Papa Don't Preach

Duration	4'06"
BPM/time signature	122/$\frac{4}{4}$
Composer(s)	Brian Elliot/additional lyrics by Madonna
Original album	*True Blue*
Producer(s)	Madonna/Stephen Bray
Remixed for *The Immaculate Collection* by	Shep Pettibone and Michael Hutchinson
Instrumentation/musician credits	Drums: Steven Bray
	Percussion: Jonathan Moffett
	Keyboards: Steven Bray
	Additional keyboards (Emulator 2 String intro): Fred Zarr
	Rhythm guitar: David Williams
	Electric guitar: Bruce Gaitsch, John Putnam
	Acoustic guitar: John Putnam
	String arrangement: Billy Meyers
	Background vocals: Madonna, Siedah Garrett, Edie Lehmann

Song history

On the release of *Papa Don't Preach* Madonna found herself in the unusual position of being praised by religious and social conservatives who read a pro-life anti-abortion message into the lyric of the song; it gave Madonna another number one hit in the USA.

Song section	Bars (length)	Position in song
Introduction 1 (strings)	8	0'00"
Introduction 2 (plus rhythm section)	8	0'16"
Verse 1	16	0'32"
Bridge 1	8	1'03"
Chorus 1	10	1'19"
Verse 2	8	1'38"
Bridge 2	8	1'55"

Song section	Bars (length)	Position in song
Chorus 2	10	2'10"
Guitar solo	8	2'30"
Bridge 3	10	2'46"
Chorus 3	8	3'05"
Chorus 4	8	3'21"
Chorus 5 (to fade)	8	3'37"

Song analysis

Key: F minor

Introduction 1 opens with a quasi-classical string synthesiser section that sets the tone for the song's subject matter. **Introduction 2** sets up the song's feel: straight drums, a cabasa part with a crotchet delay that pans from left to right, a quaver-pattern, sampled slap-bass part, with texture and harmony being provided by a synthesiser voice/string pad, and acoustic guitar strums on the chord changes (F minor, E♭/F, D♭/F and C minor/F). Interest is provided by a series of quaver-pattern string motifs that enter every two bars. **Verse 1** enters, with Madonna's vocal using her lower range (between low F and the octave above).

Bridge 1 keeps the same feel but the harmony is different to the verse and builds to a dominant chord (D♭/F, E♭/F, D♭/F, E♭F, D♭/F, E♭/F, F minor, B♭ minor, C7). The vocal, which is by now double-tracked, is more forceful and in a brighter section of Madonna's voice (F up to C). The bridge also features a synthesiser bell/piano part that acts as an answering phrase to Madonna's vocal.

Chorus 1 is characterised by the use of many short interlocking motifs. The first four bars of the chorus vocal hook use the notes E♭, F, G and A♭ with the second four bars going up as far as a high C and as low as the C below. The double-tracked lead is supported by backing vocals which strengthen and brighten it.

Production tip: Delays can be used on rhythmic motifs either to create more interesting parts or to add more rhythmic energy to a track.

Exercise

Transcribe the first four bars of the Introduction 2 bass line (0'16").

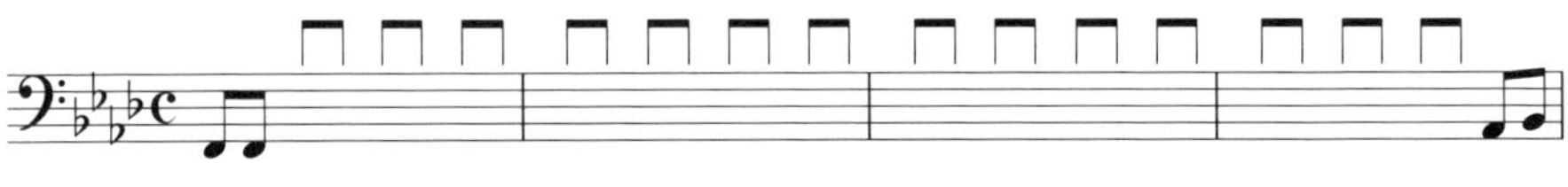

Open Your Heart

Duration	3′48″
BPM/time signature	113/$\frac{4}{4}$
Composer(s)	Madonna/Gardner Cole/Peter Rafelson
Original Album	*True Blue*
Producer(s)	Madonna/Patrick Leonard
Remixed for *The Immaculate Collection* by	Shep Pettibone and Goh Hotoda
Instrumentation/musician credits	Drums: Jonathan Moffett
	Percussion: Paulinho da Costa
	Keyboards: Patrick Leonard
	Guitars: David Williams
	Background vocals: Madonna

Song history

The demo of *Open your Heart* was changed in feel by producer Patrick Leonard from a rock/pop to a rock/dance feel and had additional lyrics written by Madonna. The video attracted controversy as it features a young boy entering a strip club and kissing Madonna.

Song section	**Bars (length)**	**Position in song**
Introduction 1	8	0′00″
Verse 1	16	0′18″
Bridge 1	4	0′52″
Chorus 1	8	1′00″
Introduction 2	4	1′17″
Verse 2	16	1′26″
Bridge 2	4	2′00″
Chorus 2	8	2′08″
Middle 8	8	2′25″
Introduction 3 (new vocal)	8	2′42″
Bridge 3	4	2′59″

Song section	Bars (length)	Position in song
Chorus 3	8	3'08"
Coda (ad-lib vocal to fade)	12	3'25"

Song analysis

Key: F major

Opening with a drum fill and a vocal exclamation from Madonna, the track sets off with a powerful rhythm section groove with a funky synthesised brass part and a synthesiser bell melody. The **Verse 1** vocal, which is punctuated by hi-hat fills, is in Madonna's lower to mid range (A to the A♭ above). As the verse moves up to B♭ a chorused guitar is added, which is replaced by a funky picked guitar as the verse moves into **Bridge 1.** The chords in the bridge resolve on a dominant (C) setting up the chorus, and the now double-tracked vocal melody moves from a D up to a G again, creating a build-up to **Chorus 1** where the melody starts on an A.

The rhythm feel in the chorus is different to that of the previous sections as the bass and a rhythmic synthesiser pad play a more broken quaver rhythm than before. The bass line is now emphasising the chord root rather than acting as a pedal. Rhythmic continuity is provided by a funky rhythm guitar part, drums and congas. The vocal is sung in a full chest voice and stays within the range of a 4th (F to B♭). **Verse 1** adds an ad-libbed vocal part and then **Chorus 2** leads into the **Middle 8**, which features a new bass feel.

Production tip: Adding a sub-bass part an octave lower than the original bass part gives extra 'bottom' and greater sonic width to a track.

Exercise

The Bridge chords are made up from the following: F/A, G minor, B♭, C/B♭, C and D minor. Select and place the chords in their correct positions below.

La Isla Bonita

Duration	3'43"
BPM/time signature	100/$\frac{4}{4}$
Composer(s)	Madonna/Patrick Leonard/Bruce Gaitsch
Original album	*True Blue*
Producer(s)	Madonna/Patrick Leonard
Remixed for *The Immaculate Collection* by	Shep Pettibone and Michael Hutchinson
Instrumentation/musician credits	Drum programming: Patrick Leonard
	Percussion: Paulinho da Costa
	Keyboards: Patrick Leonard
	Guitar: Bruce Gaitsch
	Background vocals: Madonna, Siedah Garrett, Edie Lehmann

Song history

La Isla Bonita is often regarded as Madonna's attempt to break open the Hispanic market. Madonna wrote the song's lyrics and so gained a writing credit on the song. It became Madonna's fifth top five US hit from *True Blue*.

Song section	Bars (length)	Position in song
Introduction 1	8	0'00"
Verse 1	8	0'19"
Chorus 1	8	0'38"
Instrumental link 1(acoustic guitar)	4	0'58"
Verse 2	8	1'07"
Chorus 2	8	1'26"
Instrumental link 2	4	1'46"
Middle 8	9	1'55"
Verse 3 (first half: synth cellos melody)	8	2'17"
Chorus 3	8.5	2'36"
Chorus 4	8.5	2'56"
Chorus 5	8.5	3'17"

Song analysis

Key: C♯ minor

The song opens with a drum rhumba rhythm, bass synthesiser part, percussion, an electric piano pad and a *Popcorn*-style synthesiser line playing a repeating two-bar chord pattern (C♯ minor to B, C♯ minor).

> The song *Popcorn* was composed by Gershon Kingsley for his 1969 album *Music to Moog By*. The 1972 version by the band Hot Butter was one of the first primarily electronic works to enter the American charts.

A Spanish guitar enters and Madonna says a few words in Spanish. The low verse melody starts with a strong opening gesture – down a 4th from the tonic (C♯) to the dominant (G♯) and back again. The accompanying chords repeat the chords from the introductory bars followed by F♯/C♯ minor to C♯ minor, and then E to B. These four bars are repeated with bar 8 of the chorus cadencing on the dominant (G♯).

Chorus 1 consists of a four-bar repeated chordal pattern using the following chords: C♯ minor to G♯, F♯ minor to C♯/E, G♯ to F♯ minor, F♯ minor to G♯ and finally C♯ minor. The vocal range is limited here to a 5th, going up as far as F♯ and down to B. The melody consists of a series of motifs built upon an interval of a 2nd and is supported by backing vocals and punctuated by synthesiser brass stabs.

The **Middle 8** is also built on a four-bar repeated sequence with an extra bar added to create a harmonic resolution to the dominant. It shifts key centre to F♯ minor, the subdominant, and moves through the following chords: F♯ minor, D, E, B minor, F♯ minor, D and E. This sequence repeats with the extra bar going from E to G♯.

A melody played by synthesised cellos opens the first half of **Verse 3** and as the vocal returns there are some more brass stabs. The outgoing choruses all feature an extra half bar with a IV–V cadence (F♯ minor to G♯) and a Spanish guitar lick. This joins the choruses effectively while adding interest and colour.

> **Production tip:** Adding relevant ethnic elements such as Spanish guitar and castanets helps give a song a sense of location.

Exercise

Transcribe the first four bars of the Chorus 1 vocal melody.

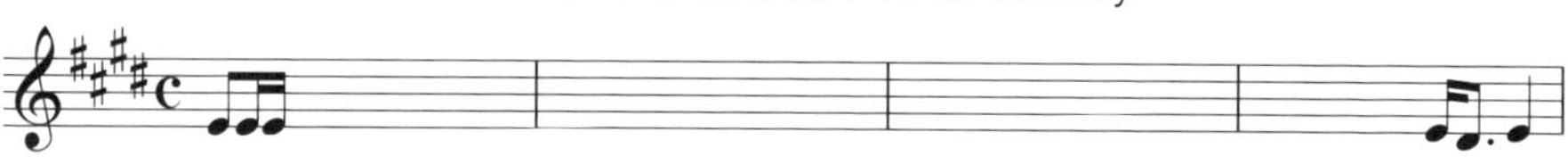

Like A Prayer

Duration	5'48"
BPM/time signature	112/$\frac{4}{4}$
Composer(s)	Madonna/Patrick Leonard
Original album	*Like A Prayer*
Producer/s	Madonna/Patrick Leonard
	Additional production by Shep Pettibone
Remixed for *The Immaculate Collection* by	Shep Pettibone and Goh Hotoda
Instrumentation/musician credits (individual credits not given on album)	Drums: Jonathan Moffett, Jeffrey Porcaro, John Robinson
	Bass: Guy Pratt, Randy Jackson
	Guitars: Chester Kamen, David Williams, Dan Huff, Bruce Gaitsch
	Synthesisers: Patrick Leonard, Jai Winding
	Acoustic piano, Hammond B3 organ, clavinet: Patrick Leonard
	Clavinet: Geary Lanier
	Percussion: Luis Conte, Paulinho da Costa
	Background vocals: Madonna, Niki Harris, Marilyn Martin, Donna DeLory, Ali Nadirah, Lynne Fidmont, Rose Banks, Marcos Loya, The Andrea Crouch choir

Song history

Like A Prayer is one of Madonna's most ambitious tracks to date. She says that it was written 'about the influence of Catholicism on my life and the passion it provokes in me'. The song's infectious pop/dance feel and gospel influence created one of Madonna's most controversial hits.

Song section	Bars (length)	Position in song
Spoken intro		0'00"
Introduction 1 (choir)	9	0'02"
Introduction 2 (voice plus organ)	9	0'21"
Introduction 2 (plus drums, perc, bass)	4	0'40"
Chorus 1	8	0'49"
Verse 1	16	1'06"

Song section	Bars (length)	Position in song
Chorus 2	8	1'40"
Verse 2	16	1'58"
Chorus 3	16	2'32"
Minor verse setup	4	3'06"
Minor verse 1	16	3'15"
Chorus 4 (backing vocals and adlibs)	16	3'49"
Breakdown	16	4'23"
Minor verse 2	8	4'58"
Chorus 5 (as chorus 4 minus bass)	8	5'15"
Chorus 6 (to fade)	8	5'32"

Song analysis

Key: F major

Madonna's opening **Spoken intro** vocal has a slapback delay on it, contrasting with the gospel choir singing an ascending three-part line in **Introduction 1**. Madonna enters for **Introduction 2** over the same chord changes accompanied by a synthesised church organ. An agogo pattern enters followed by the bass drum, hi-hat, cowbell, a funky bass synthesiser part and a sampled, synthesised double bass swell. **Chorus 1** adds an extra hi-hat part, and a polysynth synthesiser sound playing quaver chordal stabs. The vocal keeps within a narrow range of E to A and is occasionally supplemented by backing vocals.

Polysynth is short for polyphonic synthesiser, a synthesiser that can play many notes at once. Early commercial synthesisers such as the Minimoog were monophonic – only able to play one note at a time.

Verse 1 is supplemented by 'ooohs' from the choir, a snare on beats 2 and 4 and an additional synthesiser bass line. The vocal is straight in an attempt to sound devotional and again has a narrow range (D to A). **Chorus 2** adds a high synthesiser pad and an F sus2 guitar chord. In **Chorus 3** the gospel choir comes even more to the fore and the second bass synthesiser is taken out. There are also handclaps, a vibraslap part and synthesised percussion sounds. **Minor verse 1** features synthesised string D quavers playing octaves, handclaps and a conga pattern**. Chorus 4** is dominated by the gospel choir and enlivened by vocal ad-libs and timbale fills. At this point the mix allows its dance music elements to take over with a house music breakdown. **Chorus 5** loses the bass, which returns for **Chorus 6** and a quick fade.

Production tip: Note the tonal and rhythmic differences between the two bass and two hi-hat parts and how they complement each other. Having all these different elements allows a mix to be built up gradually and adds variety.

Exercise

Transcribe the cowbell pattern at 0'41".

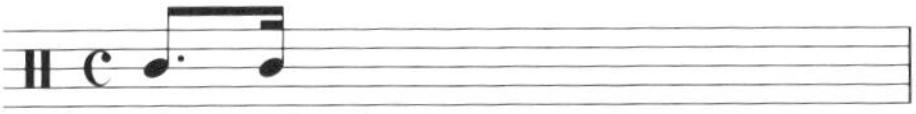

Express Yourself

Duration	4'02"
BPM/time signature	114/$\frac{4}{4}$
Composer(s)	Madonna/Stephen Bray
Original album	*Like A Prayer*
Producer(s)	Madonna/Stephen Bray
Remixed for *The Immaculate Collection* by	Shep Pettibone and Goh Hotoda
	Additional production by Shep Pettibone
Instrumentation/musician credits	Drums: Jonathan Moffett, Jeffrey Porcaro, John Robinson
	Bass: Guy Pratt, Randy Jackson
	Guitars: Chester Kamen, David Williams, Dan Huff, Bruce Gaitsch
	Synthesisers: Stephen Bray, Jai Winding
	Clavinet: Geary Lanier
	Percussion: Luis Conte, Paulinho da Costa
	Background vocals: Madonna, Niki Harris, Marilyn Martin, Donna DeLory, Ali Nadirah, Lynne Fidmont, Rose Banks, Marcos Loya

Song history

Express Yourself was the second single from the *Like A Prayer* album and its message of female empowerment, combined with a steamy video based on Fritz Lang's classic film *Metropolis*, saw it rise to become a top five global hit.

Song section	Bars (length)	Position in song
Percussion intro	2	0'00"
Introduction	8	0'04"
Chorus 1	8	0'21"
Verse 1	16	0'37"

Song section	Bars (length)	Position in song
Chorus 2	8	1′11″
Verse 2	16	1′27″
Chorus 3	8	2′00″
Chorus 3 extension	8	2′17″
Middle 8	16	2′34″
Chorus 4	16	3′07″
Coda (with solo voice ending)	10	3′40″

Song analysis

Key: G major

After two bars of an electronic percussion loop, a descending sampled string line leads into four bars of a sampled backing vocal, the percussion loop, a synthesiser squeal, and a funky two-bar bass riff. The backing vocals drop out for the final four bars of the **Introduction** to be replaced by Madonna's semi-shouted vocal ('Come on girls').

A snare fill and string line lead into **Chorus 1** which is driven along by some busy house-style drums and bass line, a synthesiser pad and squeal, lower-register sampled string lines and a semiquaver arpeggiated string line. The double-tracked lead vocal is in the forceful nasal upper register of Madonna's voice and has a range of F to B. Backing vocals harmonise the lead.

Verse 1 is a stripped-down version of the chorus with the addition of claps on beat 4 of every bar. Offbeat synthesiser rhythms pan from left to right adding rhythmic as well as harmonic interest. Snare and string fills punctuate the vocal. **Verse 2** adds backing vocals and an organ pad with a snare and string fill leading into **Chorus 3**, which has an extended eight-bar backing vocal feature. The start of the **Middle 8** has a descending vocal line with backing vocals and string interjections, while the second eight bars showcase elements of the backing track alongside a house-style piano part and more string fills. The **Coda** features the verse synthesiser rhythms with chorus lead and backing vocals. The track ends with the lead vocal singing 'Express yourself' with crotchet delays, fading the voice over a synthesised explosion.

Production tip: When there are this many elements in this mix, equalisation, panning and balancing become crucial. Keep the primary instruments/voices at the front (in this case all voices, bass, drums and percussion) and find spaces for the rest. Certain instruments work well at low level, panned hard left/right, or with a wide frequency bandwidth having been cut.

Exercise

Transcribe the first two bars of the bass line at 0'04".

Cherish

Duration	3'48"
BPM/time signature	132/$\frac{12}{8}$
Composer(s)	Madonna/Patrick Leonard
Original album	*Like A Prayer*
Producer(s)	Madonna/Patrick Leonard
Remixed for *The Immaculate Collection* by	Shep Pettibone and Michael Hutchinson
Instrumentation/musician credits	Drums: Jonathan Moffett, Jeffrey Porcaro, John Robinson
	Bass: Guy Pratt, Randy Jackson
	Guitars: Chester Kamen, David Williams, Dan Huff, Bruce Gaitsch
	Synthesisers: Patrick Leonard, Jai Winding
	Acoustic piano, Hammond B3 organ, clavinet: Patrick Leonard
	Clavinet: Geary Lanier
	Percussion: Luis Conte, Paulinho da Costa
	Background vocals: Madonna, Niki Harris, Marilyn Martin, Donna DeLory, Ali Nadirah, Lynne Fidmont, Rose Banks, Marcos Loya.

Song history

Cherish is a bouncy, optimistic love song with a Motown feel. Patrick Leonard, co-producer and co-writer, explains his and Madonna's working process at the time of writing: 'I get to my studio at nine in the morning and start working around 10.30 or 11.00. By two I'll have the music laid out. Madonna comes in and I play it to her. She tells me what she thinks of it and we work from two till three getting a structure and a form, and a vocal line that we both like. She'll then go away to write a lyric say from four till five, whilst I record the song with the agreed structure. I simply play the keyboards direct to tape, and run the drum sequences to tape off the MPC60. When I'm finished she'll come in and sing the lead vocal. She only does the lead vocal once – she's very good at that – and by about seven she leaves' (interview conducted by Paul Tingen, *Sound on Sound* August 1991).

Song section	Bars (length)	Position in song
Introduction	4	0′00″
Verse 1	16	0′07″
Chorus 1	16	0′36″
Verse 2	16	1′05″
Chorus 2	16	1′34″
Middle 8	12	2′03″
Solo	8	2′26″
Verse 3	8	2′40″
Chorus 3	16	2′54″
Breakdown	8	3′23″
Chorus 4 (to fade)	8	3′38″

Song analysis

Key: D major

Cherish opens with two bars of electric piano and a synthesiser pedal note over a Motown-style groove. The second two bars of the introduction add a backing vocal, a bass synthesiser note and then a six-quaver bass synthesiser lick (G, F♯, D, A, B, D).

Verse 1 maintains the same groove with the addition of a snare drum, picked electric guitar, a mid-range synthesiser pad and a string pad. Madonna's vocal is unforced and innocent-sounding. The last line of the verse is double-tracked which helps to set up the chorus. The verse has a repeated eight-bar structure with the last two bars acting as first- and second-time bars. Chords used in the verse are as follows: C, D, D/F♯, E minor, G, G major 7, A, A/C♯ and B minor.

Exercise

Place the Verse 1 chords in their correct position.

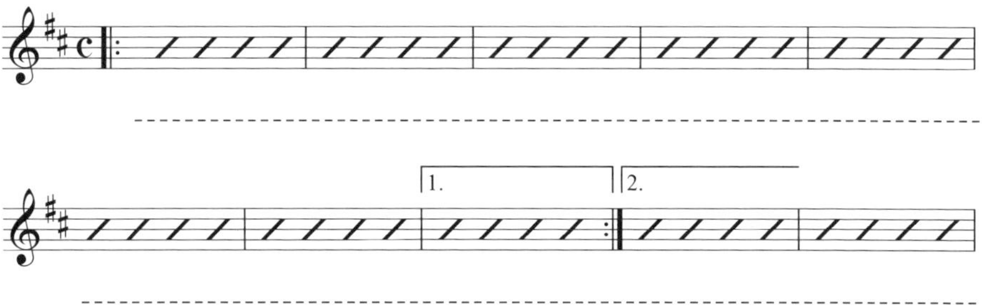

Chorus 1 adds high synthesiser bells to support the backing vocals and the lead vocal has a polysynth sound countermelody. The **Middle 8** is introduced by an ascending sampled brass run that sets up two bars of brass stabs, punctuated by backing vocals, finger clicks and an ascending bass line.

The **Solo** section features a synthesised harmonica solo mixed very low under the backing vocals, keeping the focus on the voice rather than the instruments. **Chorus 3** adds finger clicks, which are also a feature of the first four bars of the **Breakdown** section alongside tambourine, a sampled brass line and backing vocals. The remainder of the Breakdown sees the addition of the drums and a second backing vocal.

Production tip: Adding extra backing vocal lines can be a way of increasing the energy and interest of a track when the lead vocalist does not have a particular aptitude for ad-libbing.

Justify My Love

Duration	4′55″
BPM/time signature	99/$\frac{4}{4}$
Composer(s)	Lenny Kravitz, additional lyrics by Madonna
Original album	*The Immaculate Collection*
Producer(s)	Lenny Kravitz
Associate producer	Andre Betts
Mixed for *The Immaculate Collection* by	Shep Pettibone and Goh Hotoda
Instrumentation/musician credits	Backing vocals: Madonna and Lenny Kravitz

Song history

Justify My Love was controversial not only because of its sexually explicit video, but also because Prince protégé Ingrid Chavez claimed the song as her own. Allegedly Kravitz had only come up with the title, with Madonna adding 'additional' lyrics to an already composed song. The matter was settled out of court. Madonna's spoken vocal style on *Justify My Love* was continued on her next album *Erotica*.

Song section	Bars (length)	Position in song
Introduction 1	10	0′00″
Verse 1 (spoken)	16	0′26″
Chorus 1	8	1′05″
Link1	8	1′24″

Song section	Bars (length)	Position in song
Verse 2	16	1′43″
Chorus 2	8	2′22″
Link1	8	2′41″
Middle 8	8	3′00″
Verse 3	16	3′20″
Chorus 3	16	3′58″
Coda (to fade)	8	4′36″

Song analysis

Key: F♯ minor

Opening with a sparse hip-hop beat, *Justify My Love* was a move into new musical territory for Madonna. The backing track just consists of a one-bar bass and drum loop with a slowly shifting string pad. The beat is often referenced as being sampled from the Public Enemy track *Security Of The First World* but as it is not credited we have to assume that Lenny Kravitz and his production team recreated it.

The track opens in the middle of a bar, sounding as if an analogue multitrack tape machine has just been turned on at random. After the beat has established itself, a string part enters, playing a repetitive motif built on two perfect 5ths (E and B to F♯ and C♯). This is accompanied by some flanged heavy breathing. As **Verse 1** begins, the string line turns into a repeating four-bar sequence. The lead vocal is spoken, pitched low in Madonna's range with a soft tone and sensuous delivery. Behind the lead – and mixed quite low in the track – is Lenny Kravitz's bluesy, wordless vocal. Both vocals are quite heavily reverberated.

Flanging is a time-based form of audio processing where two identical audio signals are mixed together with one being delayed by approximately 20 milliseconds. To produce the flanging effect as opposed to a phasing effect the amount of delay on the signal must vary to provide the typical 'comb filter' effect. The effect first came to prominence in The Small Faces' 1967 single *Itchycoo Park*.

Chorus 1 introduces a double-tracked spoken vocal lead with Madonna only singing the song's minimal hook. **Verse 2** features additional heavy breathing and the **Middle 8** is stripped right down to the bass, drums and solo spoken voice.

Production tip: Many R'n'B and hip-hop tracks are built on one, two, four or eight-bar loops sampled from other artists.

Exercise

Transcribe the *Justify My Love* drum groove.

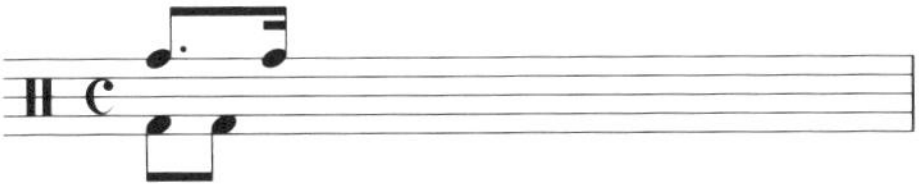

Rescue Me

Duration	5'30"
BPM/time signature	118/$\frac{4}{4}$
Composer(s)	Madonna/Shep Pettibone
Original album	*The Immaculate Collection*
Producer(s)	Madonna/Shep Pettibone
Mixed for *The Immaculate Collection* by	Shep Pettibone and Goh Hotoda
Instrumentation/musician credits	Keyboards and programming: Peter Schwartz
	Additional programming: Joe Moskowitz
	Backing vocals: Dian Sorel, Catherine Russell, Lillias White

Song history

Rescue Me was the second single from *The Immaculate Collection* and again features a spoken vocal. Madonna was not keen on it being released as a single but it was picked up for airplay by radio stations pre-release. The demand that had built up through airplay meant that when released, it came into the Billboard charts at number 15, the highest ever first-week chart position for a single at that time.

Song section	**Bars (length)**	**Position in song**
Sound FX intro	n/a	0'00"
Introduction 1	8	0'10"
Introduction 2 (voice enters)	8	0'27"
Verse 1 (spoken)	16	0'43"
Chorus 1	8	1'15"
Verse 2	16	1'32"
Chorus 2	8	2'04"
Middle 8	9	2'21"

Song section	Bars (length)	Position in song
Chorus 3 (using some Middle 8 lyrics)	16	2′39″
Breakdown	8	3′13″
Chorus 4 (new backing vocals, ad-lib lead)	8	3′28″
Rap	8	3′44″
Chorus ('Believe in the power')	16	4′00″
Breakdown chorus	8	4′33″
Chorus 5 (fade to FX)	16	4′49″

Song analysis

Key: E♭ minor

The song opens with the sound of a heartbeat merging into the rain and thunder of a tropical rainstorm. A funky two-bar synthesiser bass and sub-bass pattern enters with finger clicks, a triangle pattern, and a closed and open hi-hat panned left and right. A synthesised panpipe motif is added to the rhythm parts and a synthesised string line enters on a high E♭. The third two-bar segment of **Introduction 1** sees the start of a four-bar piano riff (E♭, D♭/E♭, A♭sus4/E♭, A♭/E♭) and the final two bars include a bass drum part alongside some heavy breathing.

Introduction 2 is split into two four-bar sections. The first sees the addition of crash cymbals and continues with the spoken voice; the second is marked by a sampled orchestral stab on its downbeat and features a double-tracked bluesy vocal ad-lib (from a D♭ up to a B♭). Here Madonna uses a throaty, dirty sound which contrasts strongly with the spoken voice.

In **Verse 1** the rhythm section is scaled down with harmony provided by a synthesiser voice pad and the piano. Madonna returns to her spoken vocal. The second half of Verse 1 sees the addition of a triangle and left-side hi-hat, a high string line and an occasional synthesiser flourish.

Chorus 1 is driven along by a full rhythm section with a synthesiser pad. The delays from the bluesy, high-register synthesiser flourishes and the use of breath stabs add rhythmic and textural interest. The forceful lead vocal is double-tracked. **Chorus 2** adds extra orchestral stabs which give energy without disrupting the track's flow. The **Middle 8** begins with a loud orchestral stab and a synthesiser pad provides the harmony while a low ad-lib synthesiser adds energy. The lead vocal goes up in range, whereas the backing vocal often moves in contrary motion. A panpipe flourish takes us into an extra, ninth bar of the Middle 8 and a reverse reverb on an orchestral stab introduces **Chorus 3** with its new backing vocal.

The **Breakdown** features drums, percussion, bass and a quaver-feel panpipe part, which because of the crotchet delay with which it is treated, creates a rhythmic and harmonic bed for the spoken vocal and rhythmic breathing. In **Chorus 4** Madonna returns to singing with a lead vocal backed by gospel-flavoured 'oohs'. The spoken voice reappears in the **Rap** alongside a descending string line. The gospel backing vocals come to the fore in the **Chorus ('Believe in the power')** and are supported by the delayed panpipes. **Chorus 5** contains vocal ad-libs and whispers as well as the other chorus elements and fades back into the storm sound effects.

Production tip: Large powerful backing vocals can be more effective if compressed and mixed relatively low in the track, as they will still feel big without dominating the rest of the track.

Exercise

Transcribe the top line from the 'I believe in the power' backing vocal at 4'00".

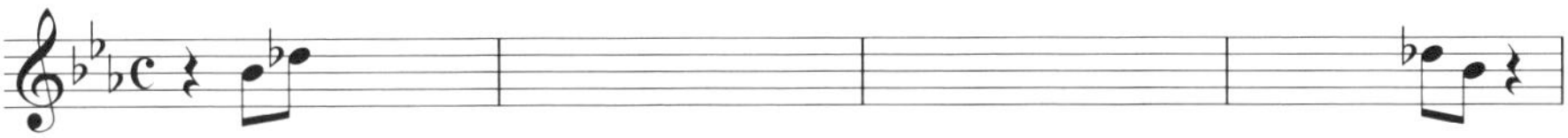

8

Characteristics of Madonna's sound

What are the common factors in the music of *The Immaculate Collection* that epitomise Madonna's sound? The answer to this question is more complex than it might initially seem. It forces us to try to pin down the constant elements in a body of work created over a seven-year period that features multiple producers, musicians, songwriters, studio engineers, mastering engineers, studios and new technologies. All these elements have the capacity to bring about radical change in the output of a popular music artist – even more so in the age of the remixer, where tracks can constantly be renewed.

Lucky Star was originally produced by Reggie Lucas, remixed by John 'Jellybean' Benitez and then remixed again for *The Immaculate Collection* by Shep Pettibone and Goh Hotoda. A process of transformation like this can be caused by dissatisfaction with an original mix, a desire to refresh a track so it can be repackaged and marketed, or an attempt to reach niche markets for which the original mix was unsuitable. All the tracks on *The Immaculate Collection* (bar the two new ones) were remixed and the results weren't always pleasing to the original producers. Patrick Leonard, who produced tracks for Madonna including *Cherish, La Isla Bonita* and *Like A Prayer*, says of fellow producer and remixer Shep Pettibone 'I think he's extremely overrated', and of Madonna choosing to work with Pettibone: 'Well, we all make mistakes.'

The one constant in the seven-year span of these recordings has been Madonna. She would have approved Pettibone's involvement with *The Immaculate Collection* as well as the choice of songs. In light of this, it seems rational to limit the analysis of the Madonna 'sound' to the mixes on *The Immaculate Collection*, and to view the album as the approved version of her seven-year musical legacy.

Rhythm, metre and tempo

All the songs in the collection share a $\frac{4}{4}$ time signature except for *Cherish* which is in $\frac{12}{8}$. $\frac{4}{4}$ is the metre most commonly used in Western popular music. The $\frac{12}{8}$ metre in *Cherish* helps to give the song its 'retro' early 1960s feel, as it is similar to hits from Motown girl group The Supremes such as *Baby Love.* Eleven out of the 17 songs are within a tempo range of 112–122 bpm and can be thought of as dance tracks. Of the others, two tracks are balladic and therefore slower (*Crazy For You* and *Live to Tell)* as are *Justify My Love*, at a typical hip-hop tempo, and *La Isla Bonita*, with its mid-tempo, summery feel. The two faster tracks are the up-tempo *Cherish* and the new-wave-influenced *Material Girl*. This indicates that dance music tempi were preferred by Madonna – not surprising given her background as a dancer. The occasional faster tracks show her versatility and the slower ones her liking for ballads.

Harmony and key centres

The 17 tracks on *The Immaculate Collection* are in 12 different keys. This is not a surprise as Madonna is a singer who uses a variety of vocal registers to create different moods. However, ten of the 17 songs have keys that fall between D and F, suggesting a preference for that key area. *Holiday, Borderline* and *Cherish* are all in the key of D and all feature the higher register of Madonna's voice.

Most of Madonna's songs are straightforward in their harmonic construction. Eight of the total are primarily diatonic in construction, taking their chords from the notes of the major scale of the tonic. A further eight are built from the notes of either the mixolydian (major with a flattened 7th) or aeolian (minor with a flattened 6th and 7th) scales. Only *Borderline* moves away from its key centre to any extent, and this is only briefly. Many of the songs employ bass pedal notes or a bass ostinato to good effect, allowing chords to shift over the static bass line.

Melody

The melodic structures of Madonna's songs have been selected or written not only to suit her voice but also to provide simple and memorable vocal hook lines, to enhance the commercial appeal of her songs. Intervals are kept small – rarely extending beyond a 6th – and the melodies are often scale-based, moving to adjacent notes with the occasional 3rd or 4th added for interest. Early songs such as *Holiday* and *Lucky Star* feature two- or three-note choruses, and while such minimalism is undoubtedly a virtue in dance music, part of the reason would have been to keep the melodies simple for an inexperienced young singer. However, later songs such as *Like A Prayer* and *Express Yourself* also keep chorus melodies simple with both songs only using four adjacent scale tones. The pitch of the choruses is often placed in Madonna's vocal mid-range, allowing backing vocalists to build up harmonies above the lead to provide extra emphasis. The melodic contour in songs such as *Express Yourself* and *Cherish* gradually moves up in steps through verse and bridge sections, going into to Madonna's higher range, before coming down again to the mid-range for the chorus.

Melodic development is featured in songs such as *La Isla Bonita.* The chorus melody is built out of a simple motif that comes in the first bar (E to D♯); in the second bar the motif repeats one chord tone above (F♯ to E). The motif is then shortened and repeated (E to D♯, D♯ to C♯) with the final melodic unit repeating the previous three pitches but in an ascending fashion (C♯, D♯ and E). Look out for more examples like this.

Lyrics

Twelve of the songs in *The Immaculate Collection* are primarily love songs and, despite Madonna's provocative persona, the lyrics are often surprisingly conservative and old-fashioned. Only the lyrics to *Like A Virgin* and *Justify My Love* come close to having any sexual content and even this comes more from Madonna's performance than the words themselves. Despite Madonna's overt use of religious imagery, only *Like A Prayer* contains any religious content.

Social issues do get an airing in four songs. Madonna presents herself as a victim of abuse in *Live To Tell*, a single mother-to-be in *Papa Don't Preach* and takes an advisory role in *Express Yourself.* It is in *Material Girl* that the assertive and independent Madonna persona comes through the most.

In a very few of the songs on the album there is a relationship between words and the melody. The vocal melody in the introduction to *Like A Prayer* is vaguely liturgical in character and sounds serious because it is in a minor key. In *Borderline*, lyrics such as 'love come down' and 'keep on pushing' are matched with suitably descending or before-the-beat melodies and rhythms, but these are the exception rather than the rule.

Sometimes lyrics influence the arrangements: the gospel vocals in *Like A Prayer* are an obvious example, while the bells and arpeggiated synthesiser in *Lucky Star* give a sense of 'twinkling stars'. These are again the exception and not the rule.

Arrangement and production

Instruments

Programmed drums and bass, an innovation of the 1980s, are employed in 12 of the 17 songs. Many of the early songs feature loud Linn drum snare sounds (also very fashionable in the 80s), seven songs use live or programmed Latin percussion and four feature programmed handclaps. A mixture of analogue and digital synthesisers is used, with seven songs featuring arpeggiated synthesiser lines. There is occasional use of acoustic or electric piano, organ, Spanish and electric guitars and synthesised or real strings, but the core elements are programmed drums and bass, Latin percussion and synthesisers.

Voice

Madonna's voice has three distinct areas:

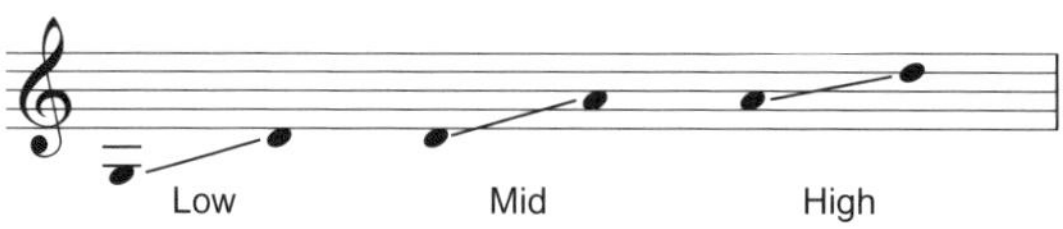

Her low range is used primarily in ballads or when she wants to sound sultry, the mid range comes into its own in punchy choruses and the high range is there to add melodic variety in verses and bridges where the harmony is sometimes static and repetitive. Songs such as *Lucky Star*, *Express Yourself* and *Holiday* sit firmly in the singer's mid-range, but the ballad *Live To Tell* is mostly centred in the lower part of Madonna's range. 11 of the songs use all three vocal areas, with four using just the lower and mid-range and two the mid- and high range. Madonna's lower range has developed over time and is more heavily featured in the later, more adult and serious songs. Nearly all of the songs on *The Immaculate Collection* are sung at a medium dynamic level with only *Justify My Love* being sung quietly all the way through. Loud choruses are often created by tracking up Madonna's voice and adding backing vocals. Seven songs use her spoken voice and again this becomes more common in the second half of the collection.

Song structures

There is no such thing as a typical Madonna song and only *Like A Virgin* fits into a classic pop song structural format. Through an analysis of the 17 songs we can see that there are certain structural preferences:

- 11 of the songs have introductions that are longer than eight bars
- 12 of the songs go straight to the chorus after the verse rather than using a bridge
- 11 songs feature a middle 8 section
- Six songs have breakdown sections
- Four have instrumental solos
- Madonna raps in two of the songs.

Production elements

There is often a freshness to Madonna's hits, stemming from her willingness to collaborate with producers working at the cutting edge of dance music production. The tracks on this album do not have the sheen and sophistication of albums produced by famous 1980s producers such as Trevor Horn or Mutt Lange, but they do possess an immediacy and energy. This stems from both the speed at which they were put together and the synthesis of Madonna's vision and talent with those of her collaborators.

Try to identify which songs have the following production elements:

- A mixture of programmed and live drums
- Placing the snare drum at the front of the mix
- The use of two separate hi-hat parts
- Heavy compression on the lead vocal
- Heavy compression on the backing vocals
- Using longer reverberation times on the lead vocal
- The use of delays to enhance keyboard parts
- The use of delays to enhance vocal parts
- Drums dropping out
- Instrumental hook lines.

9

Career, legacy and influence

Since the release of *The Immaculate Collection* Madonna has continued to tour, make records and appear in films. Her profile has remained high although not every project has been a success. Her acting has come in for much criticism with films such as *Shanghai Surprise, The Next Best Thing* and *Swept Away* all receiving poor reviews. However, these were countered by the huge success of her title role in *Evita.* She has extended her range by producing books: the coffee table book *Sex* and more recently a series of rather prim children's books. In a further extension of the Madonna 'brand', she designed a line of clothing for fashion house H&M in 2007.

Throughout this period her private life has been a huge source of interest for the media. Her relationships, marriages, children, friendships and lifestyle have all come under the inevitable spotlight that accompanies this level of fame.

Career highlights 1991-2007

1991	Madonna signs a three-year deal with Time Warner allowing her to set up her own label (Maverick) and control her own creative destiny. *In Bed With Madonna* is released. A revealing backstage documentary, it shows Madonna as a high-maintenance boss and girlfriend. It is a box-office success.
1992	The album *Erotica* and the book *Sex* are launched. Both are criticised for their sexual content and gain immense publicity for Madonna.
1993	The *Girlie Show* tour comes under fire for Madonna's raunchy routines.
1995	The *Bedtime Stories* album is released. It is a move into R'n'B for Madonna with collaborators including Dallas Austin, Nellee Hooper, Bjork and Babyface.
1996	Madonna stars in the film of the Andrew Lloyd Webber musical *Evita.* She gains good reviews for this box-office hit and wins a Golden Globe award for her acting.
1998	*Ray Of Light*, an album produced with British techno star William Orbit, is a commercial and critical success.
1999	Madonna has a big hit with another William Orbit collaboration: the song *Beautiful Stranger* features in the film *Austin Powers: The Spy Who Shagged Me.*
2000	*Music* is released. On this album Madonna worked with French house music producer Mirwais Ahmadzai. The title track is a worldwide number one.
2001	The *Drowned World* tour sustains Madonna's position as one of the top touring live artists in the world. Her second greatest hits album *GHV2* is released.

2002	Madonna records the theme song to the latest film in the *James Bond* franchise: *Die Another Day.*
2003	*American Life* is released and is her most controversial and political album to date. Of her major releases it is also the worst selling, shifting four million copies.
2004	The *Re-Invention* tour is the highest grossing tour of 2004 in the USA, proving the durability of Madonna's fan-base.
2005	*Confessions On A Dance Floor* brings a return to the dance floor, this time with British producer Stuart Price. The album wins a Grammy, receives strong reviews and is a commercial success, with the single *Hung Up* reaching number one in 41 countries.
2006	*Confessions* tour.
2007	Madonna appears at the *Live Earth* concert in London.

Madonna's legacy is as much to do with her understanding and manipulation of her celebrity as her music. Her songs have not been widely covered by other artists, and with one or two exceptions her recordings are not destined to become classics. However, she has pushed boundaries in music video and live performance, challenging the very notion of what a pop star is and can do. George Michael has said that 'In many respects she's the perfect pop artist', and her time in showbusiness is an almost textbook example of how to sustain a pop career. Time and time again she has seen off younger rivals who could not keep up with the pace she sets. Her ability to renew herself musically, create hit singles, manipulate image, attract publicity, stage a live spectacle and to move into other creative areas has not been matched or sustained by any other artist, yet has influenced many.

Bibliography

Lloyd, Fran (ed), *Deconstructing Madonna* (Batsford, 1993)

Madonna, *Sex* (Martin Secker & Warburg, 1992)

Rooksby, Rikky, *Madonna The Complete Guide To Her Music* (Omnibus, 2004)

St Michael, Mick, *Madonna "Talking"* (Omnibus, 2004)

Taraborrelli, J.Randy, *Madonna* (Pan, 2002)

Discography

Madonna, *Madonna* Remastered, Warner Brothers, 9362-47903-2

Madonna, *Like A Virgin* Remastered, Warner Brothers, 9362-47901-2

Madonna, *True Blue* Remastered, Warner Brothers, 9362-47902-2

Madonna, *Like A Prayer*, Sire/Warner Brothers, 7599-25844-2

Madonna, *I'm Breathless*, Sire/Warner Brothers, 7599-26209-2

Madonna, *The Immaculate Collection*, Sire/Warner Brothers, 7599-26440-2

Madonna, *Confessions On A Dance Floor*, Warner Brothers, 9362-49460-2

Donna Summer, *Love To Love You Baby*, Polygram, 822 792-2

Useful websites

www.madonna.com: Official Madonna site with galleries, news, music, media, and fan club.

www.en.wikipedia.org/wiki/Madonna: General information on Madonna.

www.madonnadiscography.com: A complete Madonna discography with over 1,500 items listed.

10
Technical glossary

Agogo: A Latin American percussion instrument with African roots. Two high-pitched conical metal cowbells are attached on either end of a U-shaped piece of metal and then hit with a stick.

Analogue: Analogue technology uses a continuously varying signal rather than the stream of numbers generated by a digital signal. Analogue recording technology refers to tape-based recorders that shift magnetic particles on the tape to create an analogue of the original waveform.

Automated mixing: Automation of faders, panning, mute switches and many other elements are features of mixing consoles with automated mixing. Mix settings can be stored for future recall.

Cabasa: A Latin American percussion instrument that has several chains of steel balls wrapped around a small wooden cylinder to make a sound similar to that of a rattlesnake. Its long handle can be shaken to give a lengthy rattle or (with the other hand dampening the steel balls) twisted to provide a short cut sound.

Compression: A method of controlling the dynamics of a signal by bringing down the amount of level increase in louder sections. This can be used to create a smoother dynamic so louder sounds don't jump out, or to create rhythmic emphasis by highlighting the quieter parts of a signal.

Delay: A delay device allows a signal to be repeated after the original signal has been heard. The time between the original and the delays, the number of delays and the rate at which they fade can all be controlled.

Digital: Digital recorders sample snapshots of sound and store the resulting information as numbers.

Dry: Without reverberation.

Envelope: An envelope normally consists of attack, decay, sustain and release parameters. These can be used to control amplitude (loudness) or tone (filter). A major component for shaping the sound on a synthesiser but also found as a stand-alone processing unit.

Filter: A filter controls the brightness and resonance of a sound. A major component for shaping the sound on a synthesiser but also found as a stand-alone processing unit.

Frequency modulation (FM): A method of synthesis using frequency modulation tone generators.

Linear Arithmetic Wavetable Synthesis: A method of synthesis using computational techniques of linear arithmetic.

Loop: A repeated sample that is used as the basis for a section of a track.

MIDI: Musical Instrument Digital Interface, the standard digital format for connecting all electronic instruments and computers. This allows devices to 'talk' to each other. Note information and other performance information can be stored and then edited in a sequencer.

Mixolydian scale: A major scale with a flattened 7th.

Noise gate: Used to remove background noise on a recorded track before it starts and during breaks in performance.

Oscillator: An oscillator is an electronic circuit that oscillates to produce a pitched tone that can then be shaped by other controllers on a synthesiser.

Pad: A three- or four-note sustained chord whose only function is to provide texture and mark any changes of harmony.

Polyphonic: The ability to play many notes at a time on a synthesiser or keyboard.

Reverberation (reverb): The addition of reverberation places a sound in a space.

Salsa clave: A two-bar rhythmic pattern that is the foundation of the Cuban salsa style. It is often played on a percussion instrument also known as the clave (two resonant wooden blocks, hit together) and comes in two forms: the 2-3 and the 3-2 clave.

Sampler: A digital sound recorder that acts as a sound source for the playback of samples.

Sequencer: A hardware or software device that stores, edits and plays back MIDI note information. The sequencer does not store the sounds themselves.

Signal processing: The process of adding effects to an audio signal.

Slapback: A length of delay that adds an audible single repeat after the initial signal.

Soundfield: The sonic space which a recording occupies.

Synchronisation: To lock together two or more devices (often a sequencer and tape machine).

Synthesiser: An electronic sound-producing device that manipulates waveforms created by onboard sound sources.

Vari-speed: The process of speeding up a tape player by a small amount to make a track sound faster and tighter.

Wet: With the addition of reverberation.